T0082851

ECONOMICS FOR A HEALTHY PLANET

THE SMALL BOOK WITH BIG IDEAS

IAIN MILLER

authorHOUSE®

AuthorHouse™ UK
1663 Liberty Drive
Bloomington, IN 47403 USA
www.authorhouse.co.uk
Phone: UK TFN: 0800 0148641 (Toll Free inside the UK)
UK Local: 02036 956322 (+44 20 3695 6322 from outside the UK)

Published by AuthorHouse 16th April 2021

ISBN: 978-1-6655-8816-4 (sc)
ISBN: 978-1-6655-8814-0 (hc)
ISBN: 978-1-6655-8815-7 (e)

Print information available on the last page.

This book is printed on acid-free paper.

CONTENTS

ACKNOWLEDGEMENTS

My daughter Izzy was an inspiration for this book. At the age of fourteen, she started to attend climate change marches, leading the group attending from her school, and speaking on the local TV station. I had long talked the talk on such issues with her and was in awe of what she was doing. But what was I doing? Wrapped up in my own bubble of full-time employment in the banking industry, I had little time to devote to such causes. I may have made the odd charitable donation and signed a few petitions, but the reality was that in Izzy's short life, she had already done more than I had to support environmental causes. I decided it was time for me to take action.

Izzy has also done an amazing job of helping me to shape the book, correct my grammar, and (with her grasp of the English language being so much better than mine) make it more readable.

Many of the ideas in this book come from Anastasia, who lives deep in the remote Siberian wilderness. Her extraordinary powers and knowledge far exceed anything known today and have been documented in a series of books by Vladimir Megre. I cannot thank them enough for sharing their experiences and insight into the natural world. Truly inspirational, you will hear more about them in this book.

Other world leaders in the environmental movement, such as environmental activist Gretta Thunberg, broadcaster and natural historian Sir David Attenborough, economist Kate Raworth, author Isabella Tree, and her conservationist husband Charlie Burrell have very much helped me to shape my thoughts for this book.

Thanks must also go to Ed Elliot and to my mum, Joanna Miller, for proofreading my book and giving valuable feedback, to Billy Langdown for creating the cover of this book, to Drew Graves and Ethan Strudwick for producing short videos to explain parts of the book, to AuthorHouse for making the publishing of this book a reality, and last but not least to my wife, Rach, who as always supports me wholeheartedly in all of my projects.

CHAPTER 1

INTRODUCTION

Today we have economies that need to grow, whether or
not they make us thrive: what we need are economies
that make us thrive, whether or not they grow.
—Kate Raworth, *Doughnut Economics*[1]

For as long as I can remember, I've been fascinated by money: how it works, where it comes from, and ultimately, how we can make more of it. You could say I was almost obsessed, addicted even. I was a slave to this ever-hungry capitalist within me, satisfied only by the rising figures of my bank balance. For me, one of the most thrilling aspects of capitalism was the idea that once you had made some money, you could then invest it to earn a return. This only exacerbated my need to earn more, making the whole thing into a vicious circle of earning and investing. I was much like the user of any addictive substance, always taking more in attempt to experience that elusive first high once again. Thinking about it now, I realise perhaps it *was* an addiction; after all, the rush I felt from a lump sum that would very marginally affect my standard of living was a little

[1] Kate Raworth, *Doughnut Economics: Seven Ways to Think Like a 21st-Century Economist.*

disproportionate. However, society has always convinced me it was a healthy addiction; if I made money, then I must be adding value to the economy, as people were willing to pay for the goods or services I was offering.

Whether it was providing finance, accommodation, or expertise, I was (supposedly) enhancing the lives of others. However, I have become convinced that this was not necessarily always the case.

If you were to ask me how it began, I would have to ask you to imagine a schoolboy named Tony Higgins. Tony was always happy, always smiling, and he had a rather cheeky disposition. He also liked his food, particularly layer cakes and jam pasties that were sold at the school canteen. He would usually spend most of his dinner money at lunchtime, so at break, when he wanted his layer cake or jam pasty, he'd come bouncing up to me with a huge grin on his face to say, "Hey Miller, lend me 50p, and I'll give ya a quid tomorrow."

Well, that was a deal that I couldn't refuse. I might not get the quid the next day, but it would be more than 50p, so I was very happy with my return. The idea of 100 per cent interest on my loan was an opportunity that could not be missed. That was, until the last week of school.

He was about to pay me back a pound for the 50p I had lent him, but then Andrew Parsons said, "Don't give it to him; he's made enough money out of you."

Tony agreed and with a big grin told me to do one.

I smiled and said, "Fair enough"; it had been good for a while, and this was fair game. If you take risks with your money, you have to accept you will lose some deals.

Then when I got to sixth form, I started studying economics. I took an interest in the financial press and started turning my pocket money into stocks and shares. I studied accountancy and finance at Heriot-Watt University and then embarked on a career in the financial services industry, spending over twenty years in investment banking. But it wasn't all just financial services; I also saw the attraction of investing in property and quickly became far more familiar with the term *mortgage* than a man in his early twenties should be; I had three of them by the age of twenty-four. It became abundantly clear that I really enjoyed making money, and I soon found a wife who loved spending it; the perfect partnership.

But as I approached the daunting milestone of fifty, my life drastically changed. I was no longer a suited and booted commuter of the 05:53 Monday morning train to London Paddington, but an at-home dad and man of leisure. Now I take early morning cycle rides (fair weather only) to battle the hills of Dartmoor, paddle board the Cornish coastline, make an attempt at surfing the ocean waves, include yoga in my exercise routine, get involved in local environmental activities, and tend to my organic vegetable garden. Of course, my decision to retire from full-time employment was largely because I wanted to spend more time with my wife and our two teenage daughters before they leave home, but there was also another reason. I had recently read a book called *Anastasia*; it was the first book in a series of ten called *The Ringing Cedars of Russia*, and they transformed my perspective on life. Anastasia is a woman who lives in the Siberian forest, completely free from any human-made comforts or devices. She lives in harmony with nature and animals. To describe her life as simple would be a severe understatement. As a result, her capabilities as a human being make our fictional superheroes look weak. She believes the rest of the human race has been crippled by years of destroying the natural environment in which we live.

Whether you choose to believe that this mystical woman of the Siberian woods dwarfs the abilities of Superman himself is up to you, but I ask you to consider this: does it not make logical sense that as we stray further and further from our natural way of living, there will inevitably be some unforeseen consequences? Ultimately, upsetting the natural equilibrium of planet earth is surely destined to have unfavourable results.

After spending most of my life in pursuit of riches, believing prosperity and economic growth are a good measure of how much value we add to our lives and to society, I now find myself writing a book on the exact opposite. Of course, I have always known that money can't buy everything and that the most precious things in life, like love, friendship, or a walk in nature, cannot be bought. I always tried to have a healthy work-life balance, placing a very high value on precious time with my family and pursuing interests outside of work, but now, after reading about Anastasia, I honestly believe that not only is economic growth above a certain level unhealthy, but we should be actively seeking to reduce our economic activity. I believe there are vicious circles of economic growth at play which keep us chasing a bigger pay packet and a more expensive lifestyle, but instead of improving the quality of our lives, these circles drive the majority of us to live life further and further away from a natural way of living. And whilst our well-lined pockets try to convince us of our apparent luxury, the reality is that our quality of life is falling, and we are utterly destroying the beautiful planet we live on.

To put it another way, what I'm saying is, "We need a recession." There, I've said it; we should actually be aiming to have a recession. We should aim for a sustained period of economic contraction. A recession is associated with doom and gloom, unemployment, and hardship. Whenever a period of flat or negative economic growth is reported for a quarter, this is reported as being a grave situation for the country, with living standards being squeezed for many. So why am I, a money-hungry ex-investment banker, campaigning for reduced financial prosperity?

Allow me to explain: Every Christmas, there is a huge focus on the retail sales figures, and every Christmas, we are expected and encouraged to buy more than we did the previous year, to ensure the economy is healthy. I'm sure I don't need to explain why this is utterly unsustainable, but essentially, this means that consumers are burdened with the pressure to earn more money to buy more material goods that we simply do not need, as a duty to our nation's buoyancy.

However, if managed carefully, our economy doesn't have to function like this. If we return to a more natural way of living, we can replace the monetary world with a healthier, more sustainable, less expensive lifestyle. It will be good for the planet and good for us. For example, if we replace some of what we buy in the supermarket with homegrown produce, it will reduce economic output, but this won't mean hardship for us. On the contrary, we will experience the joy of producing our own food, the food will be as fresh as it can get, and we will save money.

If we call the economy that we measure the monetary economy, then what we need to do is shrink the monetary economy and replace it with what I am going to call the natural economy: all the good stuff we do for ourselves, our families, and our communities, but which we don't get paid for, so therefore does not contribute to the monetary economy. By calling it the natural economy, I didn't intend to imply that the monetary economy is unnatural, but the more I thought about it, the more I realised that isn't far from the truth; the monetary economy is very much about the production of human-made goods and services, which goes against nature. Chapter 7, "The Natural Economy," discusses this in more detail.

Before we get into the details here, let me just say I am no economist. I did study it at A Level over thirty years ago, but that's where my formal study of it ended, and whilst I thoroughly enjoyed the subject as a sixth form student of Eggbuckland Community College in the mid-1980s, I took it no further, so I don't think I can ever be referred to as an economist. I had wanted to study economics and finance at university, but in the end decided upon accountancy and finance, which led me to train as an accountant. However, given that both my degree and subsequent career path are intrinsically linked to the subject, I have often found myself pondering the fundamental structures of our economy.

In addition, many respected economists think we need a new perspective. For example, Kate Raworth, a senior research associate at Oxford University's Environmental Change Institute, has developed an economic framework which she calls Doughnut Economics. Rather than coming up with solutions, she lists seven ways we should think as twenty-first-century economists. She leaves the new policies for the future generation of economic thinkers. She realises the economic mindset should be always evolving and we should bring together the best of the emerging ideas. Throughout this book, I hope to provide some ideas for economic policies which are in line with her new way of thinking, albeit this book is a lot less technical than the policies advocated by true economists.

There is also an international network of students, academics, and professionals called Rethink Economics, who are trying to change the economics that gets taught in universities. Of current teachings, they note "poverty, climate change and lack of democratic engagement are rarely mentioned and if they are, textbooks recommend the same old tired toolkit with no opportunity for students to discuss whether these methods are actually working." They would like to see a wider range of perspectives, with students encouraged to form their own independent judgement of theories. I hope I am able to provide one such perspective for their evaluation.

Money Makes the World Go Round

Nonetheless, if we draw our attention back to where we started, I would like to address the ever important question: Why is money so important? Well, it puts a relative value on items, enabling us to exchange items of similar value. It enables us to specialise in a job, swapping our labour for money, which we can then exchange for goods and services of a similar value. This not only works at an individual level, but also enables corporations to conduct trade on a massive global scale. In essence, money makes the world go round; we just couldn't function without it.

However, after a great deal of research, thought, and general frustration with the problems of modern life, I have come to the conclusion that the root cause of most of the world's problems can be summed up with the exact same word: money. The very thing that we are constantly convinced will guarantee our safety, happiness, and status within society is our outright kryptonite. By putting a monetary value on things, it changes our motivations of what to do, and we are driven to earn more and spend more every year; after all, if we are earning more and spending more, it must mean our living standard is increasing, which surely must be a good thing.

In a wider sense, businesses are incentivised to produce one kind of value, money, for one group, shareholders. Of course, they, in turn, are encouraged to look after other stakeholders, and in doing so this might help strengthen their brand, but their ultimate goal is to maximise their stock market value and dividend pay-outs, which are measured in monetary terms.

As Raworth says, if we were to share things such as food, water, healthcare, time, or political voice instead of money, "it is deeply unlikely that money would invoke the very same sense of fairness as do these other things that we value deeply." She also notes that as we use money to motivate people, it can have surprising results. Raworth documents many examples of how giving monetary incentives can result in unintended perversions of our original motives. For example, farmers in Mexico were compensated in cash for refraining from cutting trees, hunting, poaching, or expanding their cattle herds. They found that over time, the motivation for conserving the forest became more and more financial rather than for the sake of the forest and the environment, and hence their readiness for future conservation efforts depended increasingly upon the promise of future payments.[2]

Through this book, I hope to convince you that our pursuit of higher living standards in monetary terms creates vicious circles of economic growth, where the more we earn and spend, the more we need to earn and spend, without necessarily enhancing everybody's well-being.

I would also like to add that, just as the vast majority of the world's problems stem from a single one-word root, I believe that there is an equally basic solution: nature. I aim to demonstrate how returning to a more natural way of living will enhance not only the health of the planet, but also our own physical, mental, and spiritual well-being.

---

[2] Raworth, *Doughnut Economics.*

This may seem like a naive and idealistic solution. The practical issue is that these solutions do not make anyone any money, as they do not create paid employment or drive economic growth. This means that there may be a great deal of resistance to implementing them, yet I personally feel that it is the best and only option that will provide a healthier, happier world for humans, plants, and animals alike.

CHAPTER 2

ECONOMIC GROWTH IMPACT ON ENVIRONMENT

Every time you buy something it has an impact on the planet. If the history of the Earth is squeezed into a calendar year, modern humans have been around for 37 minutes and used up a third of Earth's natural resources in the last 0.2 seconds. Basically to power a consumer economy thirsty for oil, water, timber, steel, fish, grain, fruit, minerals, and so on and so on.

—*The World Counts*[3]

Virtually every time we spend money, it has a detrimental impact on the environment. Over the past century, we have enjoyed unprecedented economic growth and are substantially richer than prior generations. As we buy our goods and services, we expect them to enhance our lives in some way. Individually, we can justify each purchase we make on the basis of how it can benefit us. However, we need to take a step back and look at the amount of goods and services we consume collectively and globally to see what other impacts this is having on the environment and our lives.

---

3 The World Counts, https://www.theworldcounts.com/challenges/consumption

Of course, this is not news to climate change and other environmental activists, who have for many years been warning us against the adverse effects of modern living. However, who is actively campaigning for reduced economic activity (i.e., a recession)? Most governments are still doing all they can to expand their economies, generating wealth and prosperity to further enhance the lives of their citizens, whilst keeping a lazy eye on topical environmental issues such as climate change and plastic pollution to keep the activists at bay. The most progressive of governments will be driving economic growth via investment in green technologies that reduce harmful waste and pollution. Whilst such an approach is massively preferable to the status quo, in itself it is not enough to avoid an environmental catastrophe. We need to change the goal posts for economic activity and actively aim to contract rather than expand our economies. Such a contraction in economic activity can only be achieved through a planned, controlled, and sustained recession that enables us to return to a more natural, self-sufficient way of life, not a forced recession like the one caused by the Covid-19 crisis, which has brought economic hardship and misery to many.

In this book, I hope to show not only why this needs to happen, but how we can go about this in a way that actually enhances our lives at the same time as enabling our beautiful planet to recover and thrive again.

It is important to note that even the most green of purchases that we make can be harmful to the environment. One of the most accurate and simplest ways to determine whether a good or service we buy is having a negative impact on the planet is to ask the question: is it 100 per cent natural? If not, then it will probably be doing some harm to the environment. For example, we think the investments we make in renewable energies are environmentally friendly. However, the materials for wind turbines and solar panels will need to be mined and then manufactured in factories. There will be a sales force (who will drive cars, use offices, etc.) to sell the products, which then need to be installed and will require ongoing maintenance. Eventually, the product will come to the end of its life and will need to be disposed of, hopefully recycled, but some may end up in landfill. All of this can have a detrimental impact on the environment.

The environmental impact of these renewable energies will be less damaging than the fossil fuels they replace, so it's better to use these renewable energies than carrying on with fossil fuels. However, what we must not do is think that just because we have reduced our reliance on fossil fuels, it's all good. What we have done is replace something that is really bad, with something that is bad, albeit less bad. If we then continue to grow our economies and increase our consumption of energy (global energy consumption is increasing every year, up by 2.3 per cent in 2018[4]), then eventually, the environmental damage of energy consumption will take its toll, and we will need a new solution. So whilst it's a good thing to invest in these green technologies, the bigger and more pressing goal needs to be to reduce our reliance on energy consumption, which we can do by living a more natural way of life. I will expand upon this key idea later.

We are increasingly living in a more and more disposable society, where the old is thrown out in favour of the new. This is not surprising, as our rate of technological development has been increasing at an exponential rate, and hence what was considered the latest fashion or technology may become old-fashioned or obsolete in a short space

---

[4] Enerdata, Global Energy Statistical Yearbook 2020, https://yearbook.enerdata.net/total-energy/world-consumption-statistics.html

of time. Making its predecessors redundant is one of the unintended consequences of new inventions. This will cause massive upheaval in the economy. For example, in the automobile industry, petrol and diesel cars are getting replaced by electric cars, and petrol pumps are getting replaced by electric charging stations. Whilst the new operating model may bring many benefits, including cleaner energy, there is a substantial environmental cost of dismantling and disposing of the old infrastructure.

Then with technology moving so fast, it may not be long before the new electric cars get replaced with driverless cars, and then the electric technology may get replaced with a greener technology (for example, hydrogen cars, or something else that hasn't been invented yet). So whilst we can all see the benefits of moving to a more environmentally friendly way of driving, each time we switch there is a conversion cost. Hence, the bigger and more pressing goal needs to be the reduction in travel.

Perhaps this idea is easier to understand in a more personal context. A few years ago, Rach and I decided to have a kitchen extension, and one of the most important features we wanted to make use of was the gorgeous view of the rolling hills of Dartmoor that we are very privileged to have. The result was a huge glass windows that somehow framed the endless miles of the greenery, interspersed with clusters of quaint houses. When it was finally finished, I stood admiring the view once again with my builder, Paul Edwards, who asked me to describe what I saw. Naturally, I told him that I could see Dartmoor in the distance, and the valley in between, with many houses scattered all over.

His response was obvious, but nonetheless it made me think. He told me that the vast majority of the materials used to build the houses would have been mined out of the ground. The same goes for everything that is in all of the houses: the fixtures, furniture, appliances, and all the personal items in the house. I took a look around my own house and realised how much stuff I had, both the visible and the stuff tucked away in drawers and cupboards, or stored away in the attic. When I multiplied this by even just the relatively small number of houses I could see out of my kitchen window, I realised what a staggering amount of stuff we have pulled out of the ground. If you then add to the houses, all of the office blocks, shops, bars, restaurants, sport centres, and other commercial buildings as well as their contents, not forgetting cars, planes, and all other modes of transport, the number becomes truly incomprehensible. I looked it up; we are extracting over 80 billion tons of resources from the earth every year.[5] And after we have manufactured what we have mined out of the ground for our own purposes, eventually it will be replaced or disposed of, and much of it goes back into the ground in an unnatural format. What's more, the rate at which we are replacing stuff due to our technological advancements is increasing, but how long can this go on before we reach a saturation point?

If we think about it, in the last century, we created more waste than the whole of humankind in all the time before that, and we are still producing waste at an ever increasing rate. The earth has been around for a few billion years, and it will be billions more years before the sun burns out. We as humans need to find a way to survive on this planet for a long time to come. Politicians in power generally plan for the next four or five years, just the right amount of time to get themselves re-elected. The forward-looking politicians talk about leaving the planet in a good state for our children and grandchildren

---

5 The World Counts, https://www.theworldcounts.com/challenges/planet-earth/state-of-the-planet/resources-extracted-from-earth/story

(i.e., one or two generations), but in fact, we need to make sure it's still around for many millions of generations to come. We've brought the planet to near-breaking point in a very short space of time. The only way we are going to survive and prosper in the long term is to live sustainably, which means working with nature, not against it. Unlike human-made products, nature can continually replace itself, as dying plants and animals give back to the planet, replenishing it with the resources required for new life.

In fact, most of the major issues facing the world today, like climate change, rising cancer rates, air pollution, obesity, the declining bee population, the rise in mental illness, deforestation, infertility, water scarcity, high cholesterol, plastic pollution, diabetes, and water pollution, are all human-made issues resulting from our divergence from nature. And the driver for this is economic growth.

CHAPTER 3

ECONOMIC GROWTH, BUT WE DON'T FEEL RICHER

The whole world is hooked on economic growth. Every quarter of a year, every country is expected to make more money than the previous quarter. If they happen to make a bit less for just two quarters, the huge red flag labelled "recession" is raised as a warning that times are extremely bad and will only worsen until we return to positive growth once again. The country could still be richer than it was last year or, in fact, at any other time in history except for the last six months; but the alarming red flag will still be raised if it has had two quarters of economic contractions.

Gross domestic product (GDP) is the final value of the goods and services produced within the geographic boundaries of a country during a specified period of time, normally a year. Or more simply put, it's a measure of economic activity. Global GDP is a staggering 10 times higher today than it was in 1950, and this is after taking into account inflation, or rising prices.

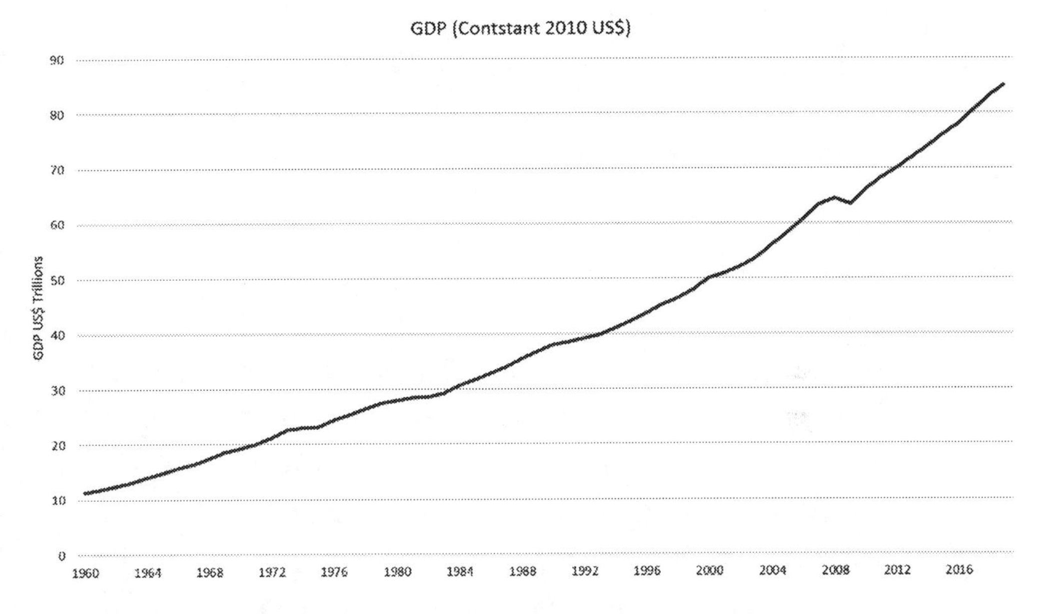

Source: World Bank, https://data.worldbank.org/indicator/NY.GDP.MKTP.KD

Now part of this is due to population growth, but even so, we are substantially richer. For instance, in the UK the amount the average person earns has quadrupled over the last seventy years.[6]

This growth in global GDP we are experiencing is forecast to continue, for a number of reasons. Firstly, population growth is set to rise from today's 7.7 billion to around 9.8 billion by 2050 and 11.2 billion by 2100.[7] Secondly, as developing countries catch up, the rise in their middle-class population is going to drive a massive demand for consumer products and construction materials as they start to

---

6 Economic Research Council, https://ercouncil.org/2015/chart-of-the-week week-41-2015-historical-real-average-salary/

7 United Nations, Department of Economic and Social Affairs, https://www.un.org/development/desa/en/news/population/world-population-prospects-2017.html

enjoy the luxuries that we are so accustomed to in the West.[8] Hence, it is anticipated that GDP will double by 2037 and almost triple by 2050.[9] Given that we are already consuming more of the world's resources than our planet can sustain, can you imagine what will happen if we triple our consumption?

Let's take a look at what will happen to our economies if we continue on our path of economic growth. If the global economy were to grow at 3 per cent a year, then after twenty-three and a half years, it will have doubled in size. So let's say it doubles in size every generation. After ten generations, it will be more than a thousand times bigger, after twenty generations a million times bigger, thirty generations a billion times bigger, and after a hundred generations, it would be 1.3×10^{30} times bigger. As it is difficult for us to comprehend a figure that big, I ask you to imagine all the money that Bill Gates, Mark Zuckerberg, Warren Buffet, and Jeff Bezos have made over their entire lives. Now multiply that by a million. Now, if the average person were to spend that much money a million times over every single second, they wouldn't even spend 1 per cent of their new income in a hundred generations. Even you are still finding this figure difficult to grasp, I hope you can now agree that GDP growth is unsustainable in the long term.

---

8 OECD, https://oecdobserver.org/news/fullstory.php/aid/3681/An_emerging_middle_class.html

9 PWC, https://www.pwc.com/gx/en/issues/the-economy/assets/world-in-2050-february-2015.pdf

If we measure future GDP in terms of today's GDP (so today's = 1), here's what it would look like over the next ten generations:

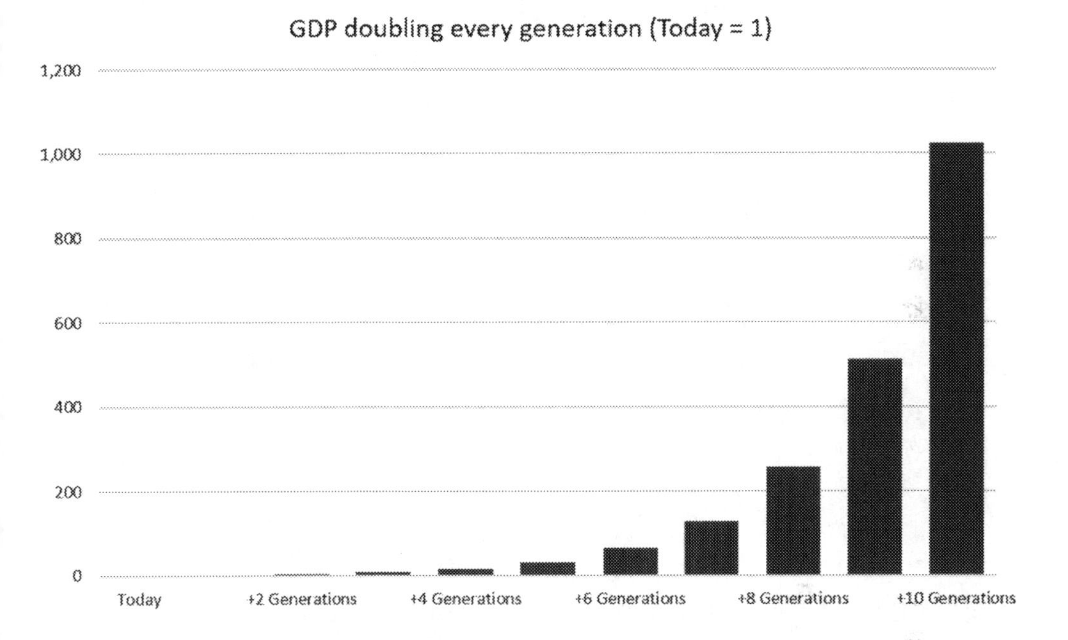

The point is, it is clear that we simply cannot continue on our journey of never-ending economic growth. Even after just ten generations, at today's prices, we would all be multimillionaires. Today's millionaires would be billionaires, and today's billionaires would be trillionaires. Whilst this might sound attractive, there isn't nearly enough land for us all to have huge mansions, even without the forecasted population growth. Furthermore, even if we moved to producing the most environmentally friendly products, the earth simply could not sustain anything like a thousand times the human-made goods and services that we produce today.

The question is, at what point do we need to slow down or stop? Well, for most of us in Western society, we passed that point a long time ago. For instance, in the US, people consume five times their share of the earth's resources, or to put it another way, if everyone in the world lived like the average US citizen, in order to sustain life, we would need five earths.

Our planet will be around for billions of years before the sun burns out, so looking a hundred generations into the future is actually not that far at all. As humans, we have a duty to ensure life on our planet is sustainable, not just for our children and grandchildren but in perpetuity, for millions of generations to come.

Now let's look at what the GDP growth has done for us so far. The problem is, despite being much richer, we don't feel that much richer (apart from the few at the top of the wealth pyramid). In 1950, most families had only one working parent, whereas today, many families are not able to make ends meet unless both parents work. Furthermore, many of us are forced to rely on government handouts to top up our incomes, a phenomenon that has never been more apparent in society. This doesn't make sense given that our wages are more than four times higher. If, instead, we turned back the clock to 1950 and quadrupled everyone's earnings, everyone would feel rich.

So why don't we all feel rich today?

Well, firstly, the economic growth isn't shared equally. Today, you can see a large discrepancy in income even between the top 20 per cent of earners and the top 1 per cent of earners, as wealth gets concentrated in the hands of the few who reap the rewards of economic growth.

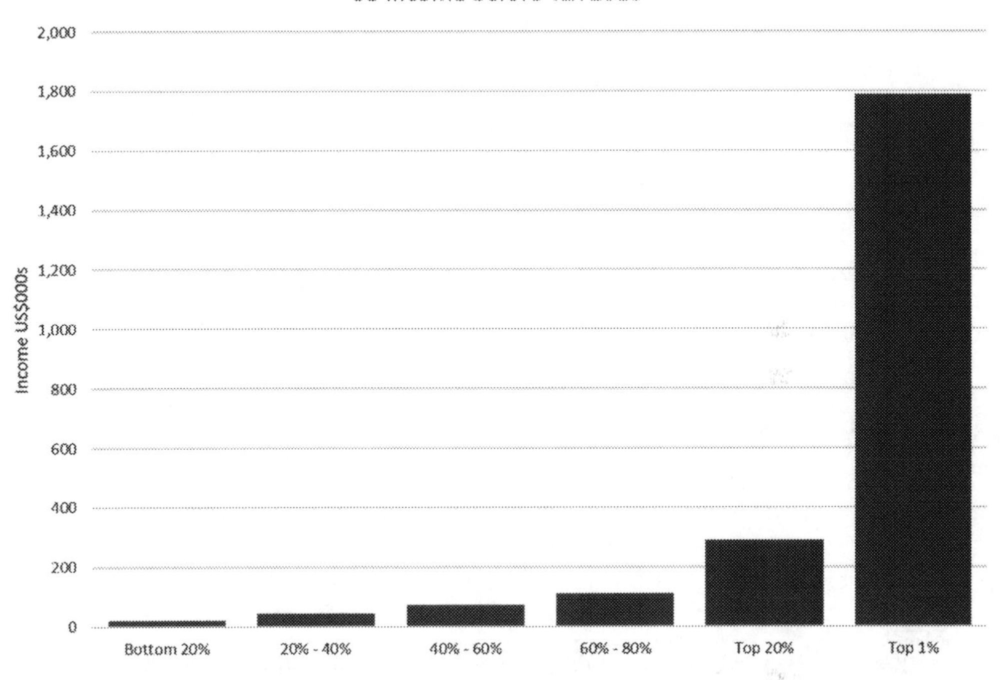

Source: Congressional Budget Office, https://inequality.org/facts/income-inequality/

As shown by the diagram above, the top 1 per cent of earners have a massively disproportionate share of the wealth, and this overt inequality is increasing with time. Moreover, despite all the economic growth we've had, there are still two billion people living on less than three dollars a day. It's a similar story from a wealth perspective (i.e., what we own rather than what we earn), as the richest 1 per cent of the globe own more than the other 99 per cent of people put together.

But why is it the case that such a tiny minority enjoy such a colossal share of global wealth?

One contributing factor is that advancements in technology are concentrating wealth in the hands of the few, as new technological inventions require a winner-takes-all business model. For example, when booking a cab, you don't want to try out a hundred different apps to get your nearest taxi; you want just one app that has access to most taxis in your area, so you choose Uber. The other taxi apps that try to be global either fail or get swallowed up by Uber.

Similarly, if you want to book accommodation, you don't want to search many different apps or websites, so you choose the one that has the most availability, hence Airbnb is the winner. Furthermore, how could social media work if all your friends used a different app than you? There must be a critical mass of people for the app to function properly, and whilst in this case there may have been second and third prizes, Facebook is the winner. Of course, there are other companies offering such services, and some of them may even be large, but the point is that it's not like going to the hairdressers, where a sole trader can easily set up shop and attract customers. This small business model can be easily replicated across a country and even across the globe. The small business model, however, just doesn't work for many of the new technology inventions that are transforming the world because they rely on market dominance in order to function properly.

For this reason, new technology has enabled a minority of people to get exceedingly rich in a very short space of time. These people are harnessing the technological developments of years, even centuries, of advancements. For example, none of them would exist if it had not been for the invention of electricity. Over the years, many such technological developments have been made, which today's entrepreneurs can utilise for free. Furthermore, if several entrepreneurs have the same idea or a similar idea, due to the winner-takes-all environment in which we now operate, most will fail or get swallowed up by a competitor. Now, whilst it could be argued that only the best will succeed, and the best should be rewarded for their creation, there is very little left for those who don't quite make the top few. Whilst in the past, capitalism has enabled many small businesses to thrive, many now fail to compete with the monopolies, and the number of people who struggle to make ends meet is on the rise.

For example, suppose there was a competition (such as a lottery) where millions of people take part and everyone buys a ticket. There is a huge prize for first place, and smaller prizes for second and third, but everyone else goes home empty-handed. Now, this may be fine for a competition; your outlay is very small, and you know what the rules are and choose to take part in the hope that you may reap some huge reward. However, this now seems to be the way we are heading in the workplace, with the top earners reaping huge rewards whilst others get very little. Perhaps not quite as extreme as the competition, as everybody earns an income for their efforts, but increasingly the gap between the winners and the losers, the rich and the poor, is getting bigger. What's more is, unlike a in competition, we don't get a choice whether to play or not; this is life today.

This trend is set to continue. For instance, companies are already beginning to use artificial intelligence (AI) to replace workers and widen the wealth gap. The impact on the workforce so far may be minimal, as there is as much work required to develop robots as there is in the work that the robots replace. However, in the longer term, the AI will get more and more sophisticated and be capable of replacing more and more labour. Eventually, robots will develop the next generation of robots, replacing some of the people who develop the robots. Furthermore, robots don't get sick, don't take holiday, don't get paid, and can work twenty-four hours a day. Nor will they join a trade union, sue their employer, or take them to an employment tribunal. This not only has the effect of making labourers redundant, but reduces costs and increases the productivity of companies, making their owners richer still. Furthermore, Martin Ford, a futurist and author focusing on artificial intelligence and robotics, predicts that eventually, technology business owners will own such a large share of the wealth that their businesses will suffer, as the rest of us will have so little wealth that we have no disposable income to spend on their products.[10]

The situation is not helped by the current taxation system, as in the UK, we even tax companies for employing workers. It's called Employers National Insurance, and it's quite substantial at 13.8 per cent. That's right, we actually impose a punitive tax for employers that choose to take on workers. There is no such tax for robots, so even our taxation system is encouraging companies to lay off workers in favour of robots. The result is that wealth is set to get more and more concentrated in the hands of those who own land or property or companies (and therefore the AI and robots), whilst the rest of the population struggles to make ends meet.

However, addressing society's wealth gap is nothing new. At the end of her term as prime minister, Margaret Thatcher was questioned about the widening gap between the richest 10 per cent and poorest 10 per cent of society. She said that the socialists would rather the poor be poorer as long as the gap is smaller. Her trickle-down economics was hailed a success. The top earners would reap the rewards of free markets, and the wealth would trickle down to those below, making everybody better off, albeit the richest few making the biggest gains. Her arguments were compelling; if everyone is better off, then surely

---

[10] Martin Ford, *The Rise of the Robots: Technology and the Threat of Mass Unemployment.*

there's no harm in the richest few, who made it happen and took the risks, reaping the lion's share of the rewards for their efforts. Everyone is a winner.

The problem is, even if the poor are better off, they don't feel better off if the gap is wider. Their ability to function within the norms of society is impaired by the increase in the gap between rich and poor.

Another way to look at this is to answer the question, what would you rather earn?

Option 1: You earn fifty thousand pounds, and all your friends and neighbours earn twenty-five thousand pounds.

Option 2: You earn one hundred thousand pounds, but all your friends and neighbours earn two hundred thousand pounds.

Option 2 is tempting; you get to earn twice as much as you would under Option 1. You do earn less than your friends and neighbours, but why should that matter? In fact, shouldn't you be happy for them that they are very well off? The problem with Option 2 is you will find it very difficult to get on the housing ladder, as everyone else will have double your income to support their mortgage application. Similarly, if your friends are going out to dinner to a fancy restaurant, you may not be able to join them. If you want to participate fully in society, then it's actually Option 1 that will give you a much better lifestyle. Applying this to the real world, it's easy to see how those not in the richest 1 per cent often live beyond their means in an attempt to keep up with the Joneses.

So, Maggie, yes, the gap does matter.

Furthermore, the book *The Spirit Level: Why More Equal Societies Almost Always Do Better* explains that a nation's inequality has a greater impact on its social welfare (teenage pregnancy, mental illness, drug use, obesity, school dropouts, crime, etc.) than its overall wealth.[11] Irrespective of a nation's wealth, they highlight the pernicious effects that inequality has on societies: eroding trust, increasing anxiety and illness, and encouraging excessive consumption.

From an environmental perspective, the greater a country's inequality, the more likely the biodiversity of its landscape will be under threat.[12] The reason being, the richest wield too much power, and hence they are able to influence government policy to further their ambitions for yet more wealth. Unfortunately, the policies they want to implement (e.g., building new factories, drilling for oil) tend to be those that are detrimental to the environment.

Furthermore, unlike the Thatcherite days, when economic growth enabled everyone to get richer, the technological solutions of today are not really increasing the wealth of the poor, only the rich, and hence the gap between rich and poor is widening at an ever-increasing rate. This demonstrates why the rising figures for economic growth we have seen over the past century have not translated into increased prosperity for all.

So what has been the purpose of this economic growth, if it is not to make the masses feel richer? When the economy is going through a tough time, politicians and business leaders will do everything they can to encourage people to spend and consume more to get the economy going again. If you can afford to go shopping, it almost feels like your moral duty to spend and keep struggling businesses going. Whilst this is understandable (after all, people will lose their jobs if businesses can't survive), we do need to take a good look at what we are doing. Is it right that even if we don't need something,

---

[11] Wilkinson and Pickett, *The Spirit Level.*

[12] National Library of Medicine, https://pubmed.ncbi.nlm.nih.gov/19765041/

we should consume more than we did last year because other people's jobs depend on it?

We can think of economic growth and technological advancements as junk food for the planet. We crave the junk food, so every month, we feed our planet with more and more junk food. Eventually, we realise that junk food is making both us and the planet sick, so we try to change the diet to become healthier (e.g., invest in green technology). However, despite these efforts, we still feed it more every month, and the health problems continue to get worse.

We add to GDP every time we create something of monetary value, the idea being, this value creation has made us better off and hence the measurement of value creation, GDP, goes up. If we add to GDP when we create value, shouldn't we deduct from GDP when we destroy value? For example, if we go out and buy a brand-new car, we add to GDP. Now let's say the next day, you are involved in a terrible accident. Fortunately, you get away with minor injuries, but the car is a write-off. The emergency services are called to the scene to deal with the situation. You get taken to hospital to get treatment for your minor injuries, and what's left of the car is taken away to be disposed of, and the road is cleared of debris. You are insured, so you are able to go out and buy another brand-new car. The work of the emergency services, the hospital, and the clean-up and disposal operations all add to GDP. Add that to the purchase of the second car, and compared with just buying the one car and having no accident, the GDP value recorded has more than doubled as a result of the accident. So current economic thinking would have us believe that we are better off when we destroy value like this, but in fact, we are much worse off.

The GDP goal encourages a disposable society, throwing away value only to replace it with something new. As with the car example, if we have some goods which are getting a bit old or just outdated, the pursuit of economic growth encourages us to throw them away and buy a brand-new replacement. The same applies on a much bigger scale; disasters such as hurricanes, floods, and earthquakes result in rebuilding the things that got destroyed, often adding many billions to GDP. Also, large infrastructure projects by governments, replacing old infrastructure with new, will add many billions to GDP. Not only do we not deduct the value we are destroying in our GDP metric, we do not deduct anything for the environmental damage it creates.

The GDP goal also promotes overproduction and waste. For example, according to the UN Food and Agriculture Organisation, roughly one-third of the food produced in the world for human consumption every year (1.3 billion tonnes) gets lost or wasted.[13] Yet the food and farming industry doesn't want to address this for fear of driving itself out of business.

The first of Raworth's seven ways to think like a twenty-first-century economist tells us to "Change the Goal." She explains how in the twentieth century, we lost our goal by chasing economic growth, pushing many societies into deepening inequality, and sending all of us towards economic collapse.

We need to take a step back. Rather than trying unquestionably to chase ever more GDP growth, we need to ask whether this is the right direction for the human race. From the above analysis, I hope I have convinced you that GDP growth is not in fact increasing the

---

[13] Food and Agriculture Organization of the United Nation, "Cutting Food Waste to Feed the World," http://www.fao.org/news/story/en/item/74192/icode/

actual wealth of the masses, but rather the wealth of the top 1 percent. It is evident that the goal of increasing GDP is no longer aligned with the goal of enhancing welfare for the majority; this has many unfavourable consequences on society and the planet.

CHAPTER 4

THE VICIOUS CIRCLES

In this chapter, I would like to demonstrate that there are several vicious circles of economic growth at play, where the more we grow our economies, the more we need to continue growing them. This has enabled the rich to get richer whilst the struggle for the poor to make ends meet only increases. Three such vicious circles are outlined here, but I'm sure many others exist.

Vicious Circle 1. Property Prices

So as we've discussed, the more economic growth we have, the more wealth gets concentrated in the hands of the few. These wealthy people need somewhere to put their money. Generally, the very rich don't spend their entire income, and hence they will look for investments. The two main asset classes they invest in are businesses and property. Business investments typically consist of either ploughing the profits they have made back into their own business or investing in other businesses, such as stock market investments or private stakes in their wealthy friends' businesses. Property investments not only include buying larger and more elaborate houses for themselves, but in buying properties to rent to other individuals or companies, or land to develop new properties. However, as wealthy people invest in land and property, they both reduce the available supply for others wishing to buy and increase the demand for property, hence land and property prices go up. With only a finite amount of land on earth and a growing world population, demand for property far outweighs supply. This makes property more expensive for the rest of us; the cost of our mortgage or our rent is increasing.

Historically, we have seen property price rises substantially outstripping inflation and wage growth around the globe. With accommodation costs comprising a substantial amount of our expenditure, we are encouraged to work more in order to pay for it. We must work for longer hours, put off retirement, or have two parents go out to work instead of one. Whereas years ago, a mortgage would usually be secured on one person's earnings, today it is very common for mortgages to be supported by two incomes, as one is just not enough. So we are driven to work more to earn more, and this is fuelling economic growth. And as we work more, those who generate the real wealth are the businesses owners we work for. Hence, we have a vicious circle.

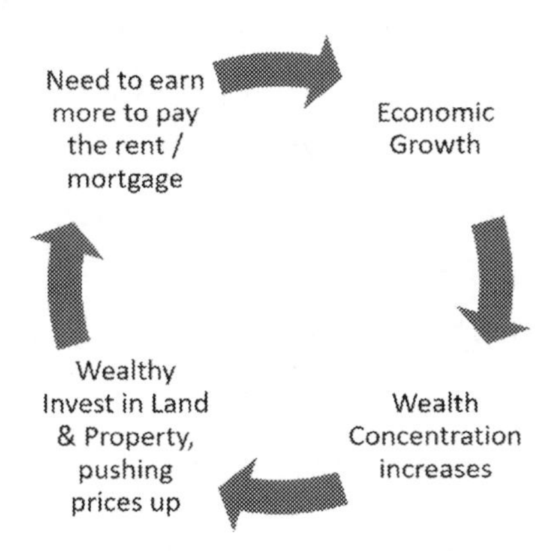

Step 1. Governments pursue a policy of growing the economy.

Step 2. As the economy grows, business owners reap most of the rewards, and the gap between rich and poor widens.

Step 3. As the wealth of the richest few grows exponentially, they invest in land and property, pushing up housing costs for everyone.

Step 4. As housing costs become more expensive, people are driven to work harder. As they take on more work, this in turn drives more economic growth, where again, the main beneficiaries are the wealthy business owners, and hence the cycle perpetuates.

Vicious Circle 2. New Inventions

The drive for economic growth encourages the development of new inventions and technological advancements. Individually, each new invention will seem like progress, as people buy the new product or service, and it enhances their lives in some way. Some people are always first in the queue to purchase the latest mobile phone, the newest model of a car, the latest fashion in clothing, and so on. However, even those who don't buy the new inventions on the day they come out eventually find it difficult to participate in society without them. For example, most people find they just have to have a mobile phone and internet access; otherwise, they will lose access to so many things and be excluded from certain forms of communication. When my dad was nearing the end of his career as a barrister, email technology had just become the new norm, but he refused to get pushed onto a computer. He managed to survive the last few years without using it, but it is clear he wouldn't have survived much longer; can you imagine turning up for an office job today and saying you don't use computers or email?

More recently, we opened up a bank account for him that could be operated via phone instead of the internet. However, when he phoned up to make a transfer, they sent him a text code that he had to use to verify. Whilst he had a mobile phone, until now he had refused to use texts. Now he had no choice but to work out how to receive the text. This year, he has been talking about getting a smart phone so he can get access to the NHS track and trace app, as he is finding it difficult to get into places without it. However, he assures me that like the woolly mammoth in the Plymouth Box museum, he did manage to get in without a smart phone. A similar pressure now exists for social media; my daughter resisted going onto social media for a long time because she was well aware of all the harm it can do to our mental health. However, she found she was excluded from so many things, and that just made it impractical not to sign up. As Elon Musk said, “The phone is almost like an extension of yourself. If you forget your phone, it’s like a missing limb.”[14] Whether we like it or not, we have been driven onto phones and other new technologies, and our reliance on them is increasing all the time.

With new inventions and technology progressing at astronomic rates, the amount of goods and services that we produce and consume also increases. And it’s not just new inventions than require us to consume more; as average incomes rise, the norms of society change as people spend more, and everyone is expected to do the same. For example, the cost of the average wedding in the UK has roughly tripled in the past twenty years. Whilst it is possible to get married for less, there is pressure on young couples to put on a show, and if they do put on an elaborate wedding, then all the guests will feel obligated to buy them an expensive gift.

Similarly, the amount we spend on Christmas and birthdays has skyrocketed. Nowadays, at a children’s birthday party, not only are the

---

[14] Business Insider, https://www.businessinsider.com/elon-musk-humans-must-become-cyborgs-to-compete-with-ai-2019-8?r=US&IR=T#:~:text=%22We%20are%20already%20a%20cyborg,it's%20like%20a%20missing%20limb.

guests expected to bring the birthday boy or girl a nice gift, the host is expected to give all the guests a party bag to go home with. Much of this gift exchange will end up in landfill within a few days or weeks, but there is still such an expectation to comply with the norms of modern-day society. We have created a disposable society that adds to the GDP and strains the environment, but does not create any meaningful value.

This all creates another vicious circle of economic growth:

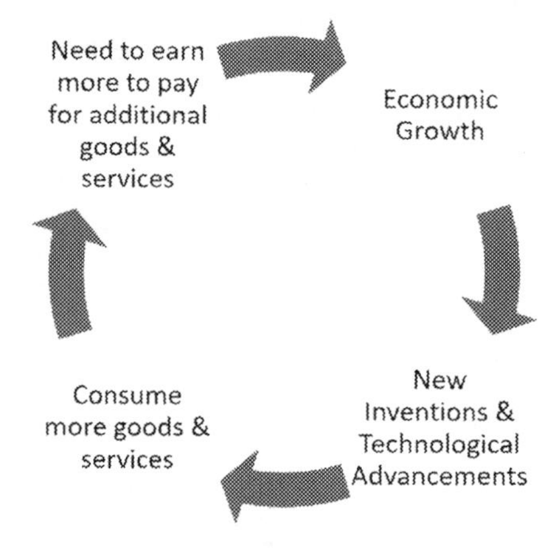

Step 1. Governments pursue a policy of economic growth, encouraging entrepreneurs and big businesses to come up with new goods and services to enhance people's lives. In other words, develop a capitalist society.

Step 2. Entrepreneurs come up with new inventions and technological advancements to sell to their customers.

Step 3. Consumers buy into the new products and services being sold. It becomes necessary to buy into the increased variety of products and services on offer and also to increase the overall quantity of goods and services we consume in order to take part in society, along with our friends and colleagues.

Step 4. As we are driven to consume more to participate in modern society, we need to earn more so that we can maintain this lifestyle. So, as in the previous vicious circle, we are forced to take on more work, which in turn drives more economic growth, where the main beneficiaries are, again, the wealthy business owners, selling more goods and making more profits. Hence the cycle perpetuates.

So whilst individual inventions may appear to advance our quality of life on a personal level, looking at it from a macro perspective, we can see that they in fact put more pressure on us to earn more, to the extent that it is necessary in order to be a functioning member of modern society.

Vicious Circle 3. Healthcare

Healthcare is the driver for another vicious circle of economic growth. The more economic growth we have, the more we diverge from nature, which can result in more illnesses and diseases. The medical and pharmaceutical industries develop new medicines and procedures to treat our ailments, and this in turns drives yet more economic growth. There are over 1.5m people employed by the NHS in the UK, and many more in other industries like pharmaceuticals who would be out of a job if we didn't get sick.

Today, real-term NHS spending is more than 10 times what it was in the 1950s.[15] This poses the question, how is it possible to increase the NHS budget more than tenfold, and yet still it doesn't have enough money? It is granted that there has been an increase in the population, the population is ageing, and we offer more treatments than we could

---

[15] Nuffield Trust, https://www.nuffieldtrust.org.uk/news-item/70-years-of-nhs-spending#:~:text=In%201950%2C%20the%20NHS%20spent,now%20a%20mere%20decimal%20point

in 1950. However, that cannot explain the full extent of the increase in spending. The real problem is not that the NHS doesn't have enough money but that the demand for NHS services (i.e., sick people) is too high for it to keep to any reasonable budget. And yet politicians always try to address the supply side of the equation by increasing funding rather than reducing the demand side by promoting healthier lifestyles. Furthermore, wouldn't it be a lot better from our perspective if we did not have to go through the trauma of getting sick, even if we are able to be treated?

It's obvious that our modern way of living is making us ill. For instance, we eat more processed food than ever, meaning that we consume astronomical quantities of sugar, salt, and additives on a daily basis. We spend a significant portion of our days staring at screens; that must have an impact on the development of our brains and our bodies, as our minds are numbed by the excessive consumption of irrelevant information, and we are inactive, as we spend so much of the day sitting down and not on our feet moving around. The declining mental health of the nation is due to the stress that comes with many aspects of modern society, such as a lack of work-life balance and pressures from the media to look a certain way.

After barely scratching the surface of a few key aspects of modern living, it is evident that modern society is linked to a decline in our physical and mental health, which will in turn mean that our immune systems are weaker and more susceptible to disease.

From the perspective of NHS staff, would life not be infinitely easier if they were not so stretched by managing frankly too many patients? For example, the NHS spends £1.5m on diabetes every hour, accounting for 10 per cent of NHS budget.[16] The amount of people

16 Diabetes.co.uk, https://www.diabetes.co.uk/cost-of-diabetes.html

with diabetes has more than doubled in the last twenty years, a trend that is forecast to continue. But what if I told you that this forecast is a choice? While some people may have genetically induced diabetes, these cases remain relatively constant over time. However, we know the dramatic increase in people developing diabetes is entirely down to lifestyle factors, so why not choose to promote lifestyles which reduce the risk of diabetes and take pressure off the NHS? Blatantly, because it's bad for business. Industries which promote fast foods, sedentary lifestyles, and drugs to combat diabetes would all suffer. The government wants to expand businesses which give us diabetes, thereby expanding businesses which treat diabetes: a double win for the economy.

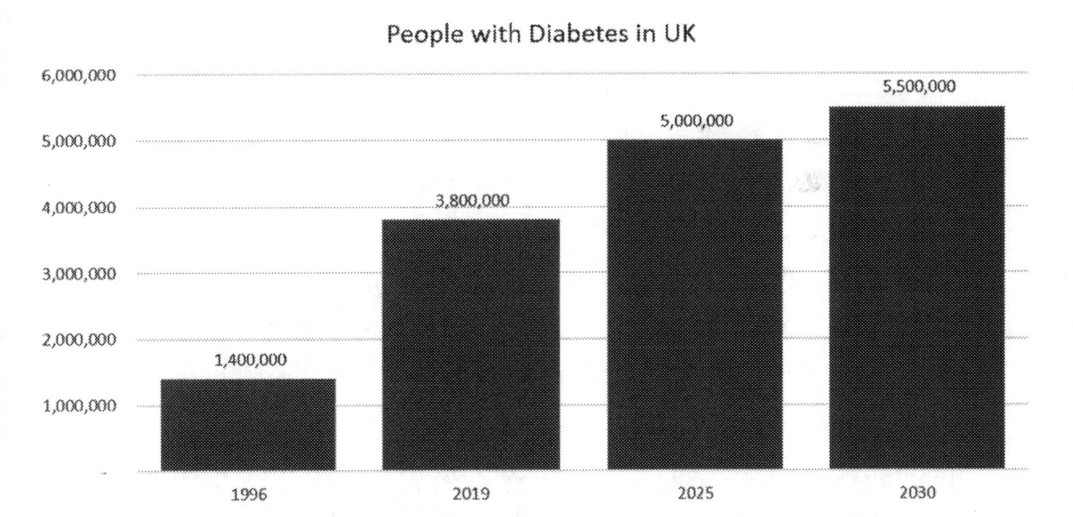

Source: Diabetes UK, https://www.diabetes.org.uk/resources-s3/2019-02/1362B_Facts%20and%20stats%20Update%20Jan%202019_LOW%20RES_EXTERNAL.pdf

Take a look at something less serious, like a cut. Years ago, people would place a plantain leaf on a cut to cure it, and there would be no risk of infection. Today, people will go to a pharmacy to buy an antiseptic cream and a plaster, boosting the economy, as either the leaf is not available or has become contaminated with car exhaust fumes, dust, and acid rain, and hence could cause an infection. Again, our policies and our lifestyles have driven us away from nature and into the shops.

In order to understand the nature of our reliance on pharmaceuticals, I would like to highlight an exhibition called "Cradle to Grave" at the British Museum.[17] The exhibition included a display of fourteen thousand pills, representing the average number of prescription pills a person in the UK takes in a lifetime. It didn't include the over-the-counter pills we take, which would have taken the total up to forty thousand. Now, imagine if we reduced the amount of pills we take by say a half, and only consumed seven thousand prescription pills (or twenty thousand, including over-the-counter pills) in a lifetime. Imagine also, that we halved our consumption of other drugs and treatments we take. This would put half the pharmaceutical industry out of business and cause job losses for millions, plus the knock-on impact to the rest of the medical profession who prescribe and administer them. Seeing as businesses are incentivised by profits, just as a car manufacturer will want to sell more cars and see the overall market for cars to increase, a pharmaceutical company will want to see the demand for its products grow, which is dependent on us firstly getting sick and then secondly buying into these human-made products, as opposed to seeking out more natural, often free, alternatives. I ask you to question whether an economy that is actively boosted by members of society getting sick can be morally sound.

Medical professionals are trained only to prescribe medicines or give recommendations that have gone through rigorous testing. It's understandable that they want to ensure any prescriptions given are

---

[17] The British Museum, https://britishmuseum.tumblr.com/post/142396578532/cradle-to-grave-by-pharmacopoeia

going to be beneficial, but there are some things that are just basic common sense. When Rach and I were having problems trying to conceive a child, we sought fertility advice. We were told there were two things that we could do to help: lose weight or give up smoking. As neither of us smoked or was overweight, there was nothing we could do to help the situation. We asked about lifestyle factors such as diet and exercise, but were met with a very clear answer that there is no evidence to suggest that infertility is linked to anything other than these two factors. However, infertility rates are on the rise, and it's not entirely down to smoking and being overweight, so it seemed to us only logical to do other things to boost health, such as eating a balanced diet and ensuring you get sufficient exercise, or trying out natural alternative remedies. Unfortunately, this kind of advice, obvious though it may seem, just wasn't forthcoming from the medical profession. Given the huge cost of getting new treatments through rigorous clinical trials, it's only the large pharmaceutical companies that can afford to do it, and hence many of the other more natural and alternative solutions get overlooked.

It was exactly the same when Rach got breast cancer. At the time, we were lucky enough to have private medical insurance and were able to get access to some of the best surgeons and oncologists. They were extremely professional and on top of their game, and in terms of the treatments they offered, they were undoubtedly amongst the best available. However, they too were reluctant to entertain any discussion about any more natural or alternative treatments, or to discuss what lifestyle factors may have led to the cancer. To be fair in Rach's case, she had the BRCA1 mutation, which meant from a genetic perspective, she was extremely likely to develop breast cancer, and her genes could be used to explain why she got it. However, it wasn't a 100 per cent guarantee that she would get it, so there must be something different between why Rach got it and others with the same gene didn't, but the professionals thought that kind of discussion was a waste of time.

She tried many different things to boost her chances of a full recovery, such as dietary changes, eating organic, juicing wheatgrass, cranial sacral therapy, spiritual healing, reiki, and meditation. Whilst it's impossible to scientifically prove the effectiveness of any of these treatments, the recommendations of a spiritual healer undoubtedly saved her life. Rach had a number of cists on both her left and right breasts, which were picked up by ultrasound. It was the one on the left that had a suspicious looking lump, so the surgeon operated to remove it. Rach was worried about the cists on her right breast, and went to see a spiritual healer. The healer didn't know anything about breast cancer and didn't understand any of the jargon we had learned from speaking to medical professionals, but she 'asked the universe' and then told Rach that her right breast was fine, but there was a problem with the left breast. Rach tried to tell her that the left breast had already been operated on and was cancer free, but she asked the universe again and insisted that it was the left breast that still had the problem. Whilst she was in the middle of chemo, we went to see another surgeon. He took one look at the original scan and told us that there were indeed two suspicious lumps in the left breast, and on examining Rach he also confirmed that the first surgeon had only removed one of them. He operated to remove the second lump, followed by more chemo and radiation, but if it hadn't been for the spiritual healer it could have been a very different story.

The problem is there is limited funding to research the impact of such treatments, as they are not the treatments that the big pharmaceutical companies will make lots of money on; in fact, if these alternatives were prescribed, then it could reduce demand for the products which do make them lots of money. As a result, there may be many more natural ways to treat some of the conditions that we get, but most will never go through the expensive testing process to prove how statistically significant they are.

I think many of us can appreciate that the urban jungle we live in is so drastically different from the natural world that it creates a breeding ground for self-inflicted diseases. As we treat these diseases, we boost the economy, and we have yet another vicious circle.

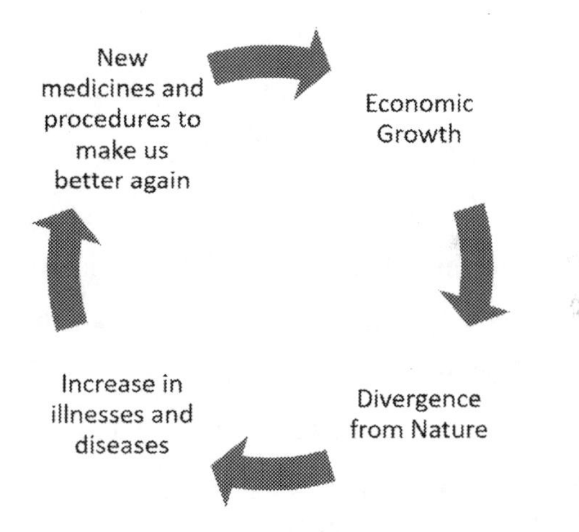

Step 1. Governments pursue a policy of economic growth, encouraging the development of human-made goods and services.

Step 2. As we consume these goods and services, our lives become less natural; we consume processed foods and alcohol, sit at desks, stare at screens, communicate on mobile phones, drive cars, pollute the water and the air, and destroy biodiversity.

Step 3. As our lives become less natural, and the nature around diminishes or deteriorates, we develop human-made illnesses and diseases.

Step 4. As new forms of illnesses and diseases are created, this presents a business opportunity for the development of drugs and other medical procedures to treat them.

In conclusion, each of the vicious circles we have discussed is intrinsically bad for us as members of society. The poor distribution of wealth and overwhelming power given to the richest in society drives up house prices, which forces us to earn more just to be able to have a roof over our heads. The rapid pace of human-made inventions puts further pressure on us to work harder simply in order to be included in society. Finally, our reluctance to use natural solutions to modern-day ailments is increasing, and with lifestyle-influenced diseases becoming more and more common, our dependence on pharmaceuticals has never been higher.

The overriding principle that I would like to highlight to you is that each of these objectively bad consequences of modern society translates to increased economic growth. This ultimately means that we live in a world where being overworked, stressed, and sick equates to positive economic consequences, which makes it frankly attractive for politicians to at least indirectly encourage them. It is evident that we need to drastically transform the economy so that economic goals do not have incredibly negative consequences for the individual.

CHAPTER 5

INFECTIOUS DISEASES

In this chapter, I would like to explore how the rise of new diseases in recent years is in fact a consequence of modern living. It is apparent that more and more diseases are emerging that we need to fight with new drugs. New strains of viruses are becoming more difficult to fight with vaccinations and are becoming more resistant to antibiotics. Even before the Covid-19 pandemic, outbreaks of human infectious diseases had quadrupled over the past forty years.

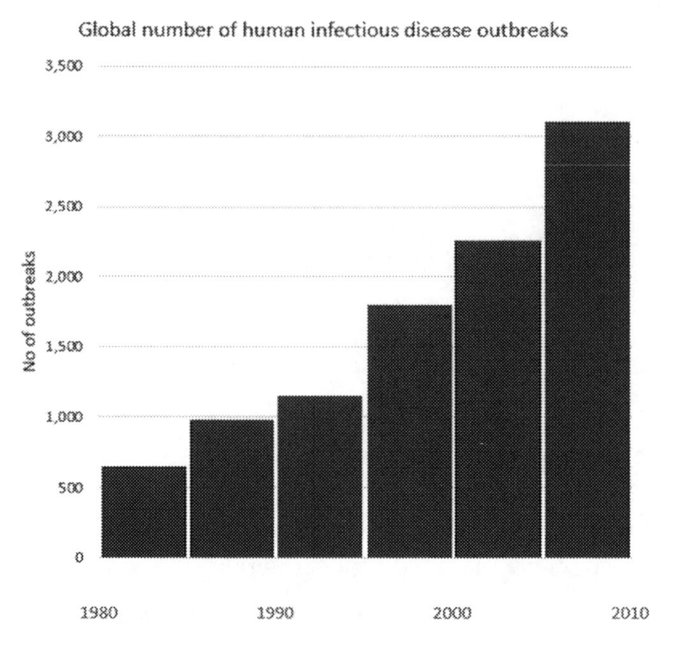

Source: National Center for Biotechnology Information, https://www.ncbi.nlm.nih.gov/pmc/articles/PMC4223919/#:~:text=Our%20analyses%20indicate%20that%20the,88%25%20of%20outbreaks%20over%20time

The responses to recent outbreaks such as Covid-19, swine flu, and Ebola have focused on how to contain and fight the diseases. Whilst this is a necessary short-term response, shouldn't the long-term focus be on preventing future outbreaks in order to avoid all of the trauma and hardship of dealing with a pandemic? I would ask you to reconsider if you don't think our so-called modern way of living has a part to play in this. Perhaps the virus is an indication that we are abusing the planet by, for instance, travelling too much (spreading the virus) or managing our livestock incorrectly (creating the virus).

In fact, according to leaders at the UN, WHO, and WWF International, pandemics such as Covid-19 are the result of humanity's destruction of nature; the world has been ignoring this stark reality for decades.[18]

---

[18] *The Guardian*, 17 June 2020.

These organisations argue that the illegal and unsustainable wildlife trade, as well as the devastation of forests and other wild places, is the driving force behind the increasing number of diseases leaping from wildlife to humans. They are calling for a green and healthy recovery from the Covid-19 pandemic, in particular by reforming destructive farming and unsustainable diets. Even more deadly disease outbreaks are likely in future unless the rampant destruction of the natural world is rapidly halted.

> The world is run by human kind, for human
> kind. There is little left for the wild.
> —David Attenborough[19]

Even if you believe that the world ought to be run by humans for humans, and you frankly don't hold other species in any high regard, I ask you to at least consider whether a way of living that sparks and spreads deadly diseases can truly be sustainable.

Humans and their domesticated livestock, mainly cows and pigs, now account for a staggering 96 per cent of the biomass of all mammals, with only 4 per cent living wild. We've had a similar effect with birds and marine life, with rapidly diminishing numbers of those living wild and increasing numbers farmed.[20] If so much of the animal world is under human control, often with horrific living conditions, it's not surprising that we get such outbreaks. According to the BBC documentary *Extinction: The Facts*,[21] if we carry on living the way we do, we will see more epidemics, and some of them will be worse than Covid-19. Scientists estimate five new emerging diseases every year as a result of human activity. If we have one on

---

[19] Netflix, *David Attenborough: A Life on Our Planet.*

[20] https://www.pnas.org/content/pnas/115/25/6506.full.pdf

[21] https://www.bbc.co.uk/programmes/m000mn4n

the scale of Covid-19 every decade, it won't be long before we are unable to sustain the way we live today. In the documentary, Dr Peter Daszak, a disease ecologist, reported that scientists have looked at all the pandemics to determine what caused them and found that we are behind every single one of them; it is the human impact on the environment which had driven these emerging diseases.

One possible explanation for this is that wildlife trade is at unprecedented levels, with huge markets where animals can share their viruses through their faeces and their urine. Humans fuel this trade through our demand for animal fur. Emerging diseases are also a result of land change use, such as cutting down forests for cattle. The diseases transfer from wild animals to livestock, and then from livestock to humans. Our demand for beef and poultry is driving this. Imagine if we let all animals live in the wild; not only would the animals be freed from what can be a life without sun, fresh air, friends, and natural stimuli, but also we could eliminate the vast majority of emerging diseases.

So, in short, as long as we continue to consume products such as animal fur, beef, and chicken in the quantities that we do today, we can expect many more emerging diseases, some of which will be on the scale of Covid-19. With the global population expanding, and the wealth of developing countries increasing to a degree where they can buy luxuries enjoyed in the West, the scale with which we need to reduce consumption globally is drastic, to say the least.

What is surprising is that we spend so much time and effort trying to manage a pandemic that, in a worst-case scenario, will only result in the demise of a fraction of 1 per cent of the population, and in most cases, those elements of the population who have the lowest life expectancy and quality of life. Yet we spend so little time and effort trying to work out how to prevent the next pandemic, which given our current lifestyles is inevitable, and which could be much more deadly. We should think of the Covid-19 pandemic as a message that our current lifestyles are destructive, and we need to find a better way to work with nature, rather than continue on our exponential journey of technological advancements.

One of the impacts of the Covid-19 pandemic is that we shut down large parts of the economy and as a result returned to a simpler life. Obviously, this was a painful time for many, with people losing their jobs or being socially isolated. However, we learned to live with less travel, living more locally within our communities. From my perspective, the more insular living brought our family closer together; we became less consumeristic and more in touch with nature. As we transitioned from trips in the car to more walking and cycling, it was so nice to have quieter, safer roads, and much cleaner air to breathe. These benefits are a result of reduced economic activity; we just need to find more controlled ways of reducing economic activity, rather than having it forced upon us from a pandemic.

Furthermore, if we don't take the prevention of the next pandemic seriously, then eventually this will cause economic meltdown. If we have a similar-scale pandemic every decade like as the scientists predict, then the financial support that governments have had to provide to boost the economy and prevent serious hardship for many, will lead to unsustainable debt in just one or two decades. If several G20 countries start to default on their debt, then there will be a financial crisis on a scale much worse than the financial crisis of 2008; there would be a deep global recession, stock markets and property prices would crash, and there would be mass unemployment. Wouldn't it be prudent to focus more resources on how we prevent the next pandemic?

CHAPTER 6

OUTSOURCING

Over the course of the next chapter, I hope to demonstrate that many of the inventions and technological advancements we have seen recently simply outsource more natural aspects of our lives. In other words, instead of doing things for ourselves, for free, we are convinced to pay others to do them, supposedly adding value to the economy. As we have transitioned away from a self-sufficient and sustainable lifestyle, to one where we pay others to get the things we need, we move further and further away from how nature intended for us to live. The following key examples illustrate this:

Example 1. An Apple

Take for example a family who have an apple tree in their garden and consume these apples. This produce is about as good as it gets: local, organic, and extremely fresh. But this adds nothing to the economy. No one is paid for this work. No one is employed. Nothing is outsourced.

Contrast this with an apple that is bought in the supermarket, having been sourced from a large-scale farm. The exact processes and procedures used to get the apples from farm to consumer will vary, but would look something like this:

- Apple trees are modified to be grown closer together; they are tall and narrow to aid harvesting. Fertilisers and pesticides are used to manage them.
- Large-scale machinery is used to harvest the crops and transfer to crates for transportation.
- Apples are submerged in water and chlorine to remove dirt and debris.
- Employees visually inspect the apples on a conveyor belt, sorting them as suitable for eating, juicing, use in pies, and so on.
- Apples are transported via additional water channels to the drying area. Fans dry the apples. Then a camera evaluates the colour, size, and shape.
- After camera evaluation, apples are sorted according to characteristics and then packed into crates; those intended for later consumption will be stored in oxygen- and temperature-controlled storage rooms.
- The apples are submerged in water again and cleaned with food-grade soap, then dried, and a synthetic wax is applied to replace their natural protective wax coating, which has been removed by the multiple washing.
- Apples are again inspected manually to ensure consistent product quality, and then stickers are added, and apples are put into appropriate, often single-use plastic packaging.
- Boxes of fruit are stacked on pallets in a temperature-controlled shipping area, before being loaded onto lorries for distribution to supermarkets and other retail outlets.

- The consumer drives to the supermarket, chooses the apples and other produce, loads them into bags, pays for them, and then takes them home in the car.
- After consuming the apples, the waste including packaging is put out as rubbish for collection to go to landfill or recycling.

From an economic perspective, all this is great. It requires the construction and running of factories, several modes of transportation, the production of chemicals, the construction and running of retail outlets, and the list goes on. However, from an environmental perspective, it requires the mining of materials for factories and transport, energy to construct and operate factories, as well as energy for refrigeration, gas for transportation, the use of scarce water supplies, the production and disposal of packaging, and the production and use of chemicals and fertilisers, which causes pollution in nearby rivers and the sea. All of these things have a negative impact on the environment. And finally, from a health perspective, the product itself, the apples, are subjected to harmful pesticides; natural wax is replaced with synthetic wax, and they are much less fresh than an apple picked straight from the tree.

So at every step in the process, whilst economic output is being generated, the environment is being harmed and the product deteriorates in nutritional value. Hence, whilst the value placed on the high-quality apple grown in one's garden is zero (in terms of the monetary economy), the poorer quality apple that is sold in the supermarket, which creates so many environmental issues, adds to the economy in so many ways.

If we were all to start growing our own fruit and vegetables, this would be disastrous for the economy, with many people losing their jobs; there's just no incentive for any government to pursue such a policy, if their intention is to grow the economy.

And yet organic apples from the supermarket are about as healthy as it gets today. Contrast this with say a cereal bar. An example of one contains:

- shredded coconut
- dark chocolate (cocoa mass, sugar, cocoa butter, emulsifier, soya lecithin)
- sultanas
- glucose syrup
- crisped rice (rice, sugar)
- dried cranberries (cranberries, sugar, sunflower oil)
- honey
- macadamia nuts

Now, not only is the cereal bar processed, but some of the ingredients that make it up are processed. If you think about the process to get an apple to the supermarket, imagine the processing that goes on for this cereal bar; you could write a whole book in itself just to describe the processing. It is clearly evident that this product is very far removed from nature. And yet, the irony lies in the name of product brand: "Eat Natural."

If we think it's acceptable to call this highly processed item Eat Natural, then how processed and distant from nature are the other things in our diet today, which we wouldn't call natural?

The Truth about Nutrition: Eat as You Breathe

Our toxic and imbalanced diets are giving us cancers, allergies, diabetes, and obesity. Vast amounts of work has been done trying to understand nutrition: what foods are good, what foods are harmful, what diets work best, and so on. As our analysis progresses, we learn more and more about the effect nutrition has on our health. The latest analysis at a given time impacts what food we eat; for example, when we learned that fat has more than twice as many calories as sugar, we went for low- or zero-fat versions of products, but these contain higher amounts of sugar. Then we realise how bad excess sugar is, and the processed products need to change again. However, we are still very much at the stage of discovering new things about nutrition, and hence there is much contradictory advice which is frequently changing.

A couple of things that most experts do agree on: The more natural the food (i.e., the less processed), the better, and a diet that works for one person may not be the right diet for another person, as we are all unique individuals.

Anastasia, the woman who lives a basic and commercial-free life in the Siberian forest that we discussed at the start of the book, has given us some advice on nutrition. She says we should stop trying to analyse the hell out of food, trying to find the most optimal diet for ourselves. Instead, we should return to a more natural diet focussed on what is grown locally. Here are a few more details that Anastasia gives us in *The Ringing Cedars of Russia;* they illustrate just how far away we are from understanding nutrition, and if we ever did, just how impossible it would be for food to be mass-produced in the way it is today.

All food that is grown is meant to be consumed by the people who live in the area. So if you travel to a different place, don't take food with you. Instead, consume the food produced locally where you are at the current time.

In fact, food can not only be specific to an area, but also, as aligned with many of today's experts, to an individual. Anastasia claims that all diseases of the flesh can be cured by growing produce specifically for yourself. She gives some very specific instructions as to how to grow produce that will specifically benefit you as an individual and cure you of any illness you may have, a process that I have personally tried in my own garden, and am pleased to say I am in very good health. A summary of the process is as follows, although a more detailed explanation can be found in the books by Vladimir Meagre (it is described in book 1, *Anastasia,* and repeated in some of the later books):[22]

- Before you plant a seed, put it in your mouth and hold it under your tongue, for at least nine minutes.
- Then place the seed between the palm of your hands and blow on it gently, whilst standing barefoot on the spot where you will plant the seed.
- Next, hold it with your hands open, presenting the seed to the universe.
- After planting the seed, do not water it for three days so that your saliva is not washed away.

Anastasia claims that when a seed is planted in this way, during its cultivation, it will pick up the energies it needs from the earth and the universe for a given individual.

One other aspect that Anastasia talks about is the process and the thought of growing produce. Using machinery to cultivate our crops is very detrimental to them. Here is a parable:

The Smith family have achieved complete self-sufficiency. They produce all their own food, living off their land. Their next-door

---

22 Vladimir Megre, *The Ringing Cedars of Russia* series of books.

neighbours, the Joneses, have done the same. Both families are completely in tune with nature, and are happy and healthy. The Joneses invite the Smiths round for dinner, and the Smiths comment that their tomatoes are particularly tasty. They have a wonderful evening, and at the end, the Smiths leave with a big box of tomatoes and invite the Joneses round for dinner the following week. A week later, they have an equally splendid evening, and the Joneses comment that their potatoes are particularly tasty, and end up leaving with a big box of potatoes.

So far, so good; they each have given the other some of their own produce, which they are proud of and would like the other to enjoy. Then they get chatting and come up with the idea that the Smiths produce more potatoes and less other produce, and the Joneses produce more tomatoes and less other produce. This way, they can sell their excess tomatoes and potatoes, and because they are so delicious, they can sell them for a high price, enough to buy them the produce they are no longer growing and have some money left over to spend on other things.

It seems like a great business plan; Ricardo's theory of comparative advantage,[23] at its simplest. However, what it doesn't take into account is that whilst the physical tasks of growing the produce may be identical to what it was before, the thought or motivation for growing the produce has changed. It is no longer grown for the benefit of themselves or their loved ones, but grown for what it can be exchanged for. Instead of wondering how the produce will taste, how it will nourish their bodies, or how it will delight their friends,

---

[23] David Ricardo was a nineteenth-century British economist who attributed the cause and benefits of international trade to the differences in the relative opportunity costs (costs in terms of other goods given up) of producing the same commodities among countries.

they are asking, "What will this sell for?" and "What can I buy with the proceeds?" According to Anastasia, this change of thought will reduce the quality and nutritional value of the produce.

If this is to be believed, it shows just how far away we are from understanding nutrition, but we are a very long way from being able to prove, or disprove, Anastasia's advice. When she talks about energy, she is not talking about the calorific value that we measure, but an energy that we are unable to quantify in scientific terms. For example, how do you measure love, the most powerful energy in the universe? We are light-years away from understanding the true value of the nutrition found in the food we eat, which is specific to an individual.

I realise that Anastasia's ideas might be a bit far-fetched for some. However, I ask you to think about how much conflicting information there is about nutrition, and observe how different diets will work for some people more than others. There are already books about eating right for your blood type and body type, and for those with underlying health issues, which makes sense given we are all unique individuals. Is it not therefore plausible that nutrition could be specific to the individual, such that we were designed to eat the produce that was grown locally, or even better the produce that was grown by us?

The problem is, this involves time and effort (and some land) at an individual level, so we can't outsource the task and pay for someone else to grow it for us. Likewise, there is no business opportunity here, no opportunity to make money out of this. If we were all to start growing our own food, only for ourselves and our loved ones, this would destroy the food industry from farmers to manufacturers, from wholesalers to retailers, from restaurants to delivery services. Furthermore, it would destroy much of the healthcare services, as there would be much less illness as we reap the health benefits from nutritious food and the exercise from tending to our gardens. It would be disastrous for the economy. Many would lose their jobs. But then, if we don't need to buy food or pay for so much healthcare, we wouldn't need to work so much, not to mention the added benefits to our quality of life of feeling happier, healthier, and less lethargic.

We consume three meals a day: breakfast, lunch, and dinner (well, most of us do). We have a plethora of cookery books, magazines, and TV programmes telling us how to prepare our food, for consumption in one of our daily meals. We either spend a fair bit of time preparing our meals, or we buy in food that has already been made to speed the process up. However, according to Anastasia, if we were to live in a natural world, free from our artificial inventions, and living as nature intended us to live, then eating would become part of our subconscious processes. If we saw something that we would like to eat, such as a berry, we would pick it and eat it. It would be completely fresh. The universe will have timed the consumption of the berry down to the millisecond.

For example, when you are out for a walk and see a berry and think, *That looks nice*, then that is the time you should be eating it, not five days later, after it's been shipped around the world before ending up in your fridge. All the food we need to eat should be available to us as and when we needed it. Anastasia says we would have more time to focus on more important things than eating (although I'm not sure she appreciates just how much satisfaction we get from eating; LOL), and that eating should be as natural as breathing, hence her expression "Eat as you breathe."

The "Eat as you breathe" option isn't readily available to those of us living in modern society. However, I think it's important to acknowledge how little we actually do know about nutrition from a scientific perspective, and the closer we can get to a natural diet, the healthier we will be. The more locally produced, the better; the more naturally grown, the better; and the less processed, the better. If we can agree on this, then there really is no role for big businesses in the provision of food. We don't want to grow food on a large scale using artificial fertilisers and pesticides, we don't want our food to get subsequently processed, and we don't want to send it all over the country, let alone all over the world.

Example 2. Childcare

Another example of outsourcing is childcare. Stay-at-home mums and dads do a very valuable job looking after their children, yet they get paid nothing and add nothing to the monetary economy. Contrast with parents who put their children into a day-care nursery and go to work. All the expenses associated with putting the child into the nursery add to the economy. It doesn't matter whether the parent pays or the government (taxpayer) pays; both will add equally to the GDP of the country. Furthermore, as parents go to work, they will add to the economy by earning a wage too. Then add transport costs to get the child to the nursery and the parent to their place of work, again both adding to economic output. It's no wonder that the direction of travel has been for more and more parents to go out to work, as it boosts the economy in so many ways.

Deciding whether to go to work or stay at home to look after children used to be an option, but now, for many families, working is a necessity to make ends meet. If governments insist on monitoring GDP as a measure of economic success, then in economic terms, stay-at-home parents are worthless.

The same would apply to looking after an elderly relative; if you look after them yourself, you don't get paid. Putting them in an expensive nursing home (again, it doesn't matter whether you pay or the government does) means the economic output gets a huge boost. So, in economic terms, looking after your elderly parents is worthless.

The list of examples is endless. Compared to many years ago, more people hire a housecleaner instead of doing their own cleaning; we go to hairdressers instead of cutting hair for friends and family; some people go out to get their nails painted; and more of us will get people in to do house improvements and repairs, rather than doing them ourselves. The pressures of modern life have made these simple tasks impossible for us to juggle without outside help. Drawing our attention back to food, let's explore how we can start off with self-sufficiency, where we all grow our own produce, and then look at how food production has been outsourced:

- First, we swap and barter our fresh produce, outsourcing some (but not all) of our food.
- Then we stop growing food ourselves, and production of fresh food moves to large-scale farming with machinery. We've outsourced the growing of all fresh produce.
- Then instead of making food at home, we buy food that's already been processed, so we outsource the home cooking.
- Then we start going out to restaurants for our meals, outsourcing not only the food processing but also laying the table, washing up, and so on.
- Then we introduce takeaways, where to go to pick up meals in disposable boxes.
- Then home delivery firms spring up, and we even outsource going to pick up our own takeaways.

At each of these stages, we feel we have progressed, by saving time, saving money, or enhancing our lifestyle. Or has this just been a ploy to free up our time to increase our all-important working hours? Over time, as we outsource more and more of the processes, both the food itself and our lifestyle become less natural, all the while, the economy is boosted. Again, it is the outsourcing of activities (i.e., paying others to do jobs for us) which is so essential from an economic viewpoint, but it's detrimental from an environmental perspective. Furthermore, as it means we sit in offices, staring at screens, and ordering in food, it's also detrimental to our health. This is added to by modern technology that drives us to live less and less natural lives. Even on a daily basis, the vast majority of us find ourselves watching TV, eating processed food, breathing polluted air, sitting in cars, using our phones to talk and text and send emails and use social media, and it is unsurprisingly having an impact on our physical and mental well-being.

Simon Kuznets was the economist who came up with the concept of gross national product (GNP) before the concept of GDP became a more widely used measure, the difference being GNP includes net income from abroad, whereas GDP is domestic income only. However, even he recognised that the metric was limited, as it did not take into account the value of the work that households do for themselves. Despite this, the metric has taken centre stage, and as we are so obsessed with our metrics, it is no surprise that as a result, policies have encouraged people to outsource the work they would have otherwise done for themselves, thus increasing GDP but not necessarily adding value. It is easy to see that there is an inherent value to carrying out the daily household chores of making breakfast, washing dishes, putting the bins out, shopping for groceries, washing clothes, caring for children and elderly parents, collecting kids from school and taking them to clubs, sweeping the floor, cleaning the bathroom, making dinner, listening to and guiding our partners and our children, and so on. However, this value is not measured in pounds and pence, as there is no transaction taking place, hence our economic model encourages us to outsource as much of it as possible so that it can be monetised and therefore add to the all-important GDP metric.

Above all, the more that things are outsourced, the more likely they are to have a negative impact on the environment. For example, if we order a takeaway rather than cooking at home, there will be more packaging which ends up in landfill, more travel to either deliver or collect the takeaway, and then all the earth's resources used up in the multitude of tasks required in the running and management of the takeaway establishment.

Furthermore, our home cooking is likely to be healthier than the takeaway. The more we can do for ourselves, our families, and our communities, the less harm we will do to the environment and our own health. We currently place a value on the things we pay for, but not the more natural things we do for ourselves. We need to place a greater value on the apple we grow in our garden than the apple purchased from a supermarket, a greater value on parents who look after their children than the day-care nursery, a greater value on helping to care for an elderly neighbour than a nursing home, a greater value on running outside than running on a treadmill in the gym.

CHAPTER 7

THE NATURAL ECONOMY

Human development, as an approach, is concerned with what I take to be the basic development idea: namely, advancing the richness of human life, rather than the richness of the economy in which human beings live, which is only a part of it.

—Amartya Sen[24]

We are obsessed with metrics. If we measure something, whether that be the number of steps we take in a day, the number of songs we listen to in a year, or GCSE and A-Level results, we will try to take more steps, listen to more songs, or beat last year's exam results. Whilst this seems like a sensible approach, the downside is that we can ignore things which are not captured by the metric. For instance, it is obvious that using the number of steps we take in a day as the sole indicator of our fitness is flawed, as it tells us nothing about our upper-body strength or the capacity of our heart and lungs.

Now let's take a more in-depth look at the targets of secondary schools today. Having two daughters who have been going through the education system for the past decade or so, I have noticed how

---

[24] Asia Society, https://asiasociety.org/amartya-sen-more-human-theory-development

much harder they are required to work compared with when I was at school. As GCSE and A Level grades rise each year, I used to think they must be making the exams easier. Now I know that's definitely not the case; they are driving the kids twice as hard. There is no doubt in my mind that today's generation of children have been educated to a significantly higher level of academic achievement than my generation. The metric of GCSE and A Level grades is not just a metric that students care about; it's one that every school is measured and ranked on, and over the years, schools have intensely focused on improving these grades.

If we choose to measure success in terms of results, then this is a huge success story. However, I do wonder whether the childhood experience my daughters had could have been enhanced if they didn't need to study so hard. Could they have had more time to play with their friends, take part in sporting activities or other leisure interests? Would they be able to think more creatively had they spent less time studying the academic curriculum taught in school? A UCL study in 2019 found that breaktimes in schools have been slashed and that children were "losing valuable opportunities to make friends, develop social skills and exercise."[25]

Whether these impacts are a fair price to pay for an increase in academic achievement is not something I will debate here. The point here is, by giving a single metric the limelight, when behaviours change to try to attain better results according to that metric, this may have unintended consequences. In this example, using GCSE and A Levels as the primary metric for the educational experience

---

[25] The Guardian, 10 May 2019, https://www.theguardian.com/education/2019/may/10/shrinking-break-times-in-english-schools-impacting-social-skills

has improved academic results but has also clearly impacted the well-being and social skills of children today.

GDP is a classic example of a metric that has been given the spotlight and has definite unintended consequences. There are a whole host of other metrics that measure other aspects of economic activity, but the problem with these is they are mostly measured in monetary terms, and those that are not (e.g., unemployment rate) are barometers for financial metrics, and hence are essentially submetrics for GDP. This applies not only at the macro level, but also at the business and individual level, as businesses focus on sales and profit, and individuals focus on their pay packets. With so much focus on monetary goals, as we try to achieve these goals, we do so to the detriment of the things we cannot measure in monetary terms.

We need to change the goal posts to redress this balance. GDP can be a useful metric; it tells us some valuable information about the monetary economy, but we should not be constantly aiming for positive growth at all costs. In fact, in richer economies, we should be aiming to shrink it, but this doesn't mean we will be worse off. As we shrink the economy that's measured in money terms, we need to grow the natural economy. By natural economy, I mean all the natural tasks that we do for ourselves, our families, and our communities, like cooking, cleaning, mending, and growing produce as well as the value we derive from nature itself such as clean air, clean water, and a beautiful countryside. We should replace international trade with work within local communities, moving towards more self-sufficient lifestyles. If we replace the monetary economy with the natural economy, GDP will fall, but our standard of living will not, as the natural economy, that cannot be measured in £, $, €, ¥, or any other currency, will expand. Our lives will become more natural, we will become healthier, the environment will become less polluted, climate change will slow down, communities will become stronger, social cohesion will be enhanced, biodiversity will thrive, and the world will be a healthier and happier place.

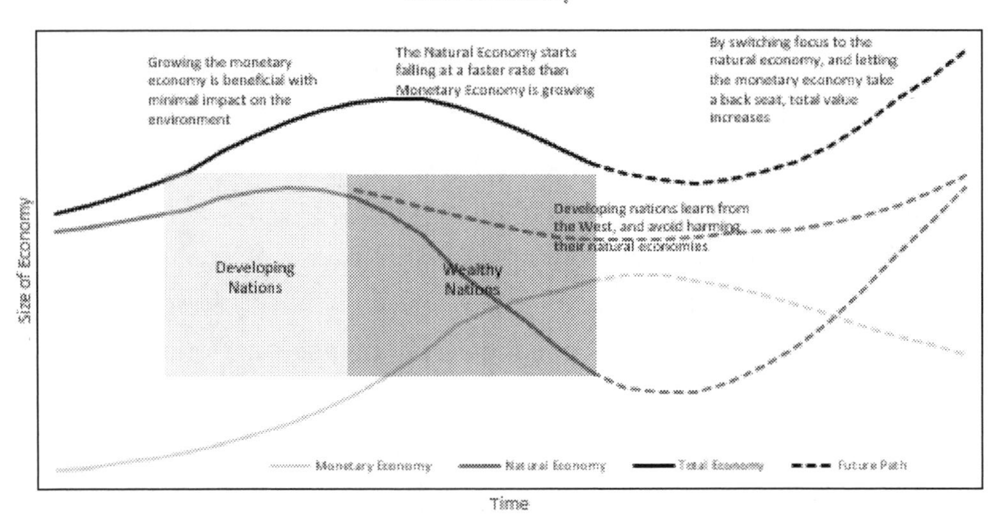

The graph above shows that as we have grown GDP (monetary economy), we have shrunk the size of the natural economy. We can think of this idea of the total economy, the sum of the natural and monetary economies, as being tied to the overall benefit to the general populace. At first, the benefits of growing GDP can outweigh the losses to the natural economy, as the benefits to our lives are substantial. Many developing countries are still in this phase, where growing GDP can increase the life expectancy, well-being, and lifestyle of its citizens.

For these economies, further monetary economic growth is clearly a good thing, albeit they can leapfrog Western societies by investing directly in greener technologies, rather than the interim step of deceptively attractive fossil fuels, and by not outsourcing too many aspects of their lives, which merely shifts value from the natural economy to the monetary economy.

However, there then comes a point whereby continuing to grow the monetary economy will have a more detrimental impact on the natural economy, hence the total value becomes less. I would say this is where most wealthy nations are now; we are doing more harm than good by expanding our monetary economies. However, if we now gradually reduce GDP by shifting towards a more self-sufficient lifestyle, then the benefits we get from growing the natural economy will outweigh what we lose in the monetary economy, hence the total value we get from the combined economic activity is greater. Of course, this is quite arbitrary, as we cannot measure either the monetary and natural economies in equal terms, but I hope this illustrates that if we shrink GDP (which is technically a recession) and transition to a more self-sufficient lifestyle, this does not, as conventional economists would have you believe, make us worse off.

This brings me to the next question of how (or even if) we should measure the natural economy so that we can track our success. To measure this new concept of economic activity, we would need to measure the value we get from doing a whole multitude of things, such as growing our own produce, looking after our families, and all the things we can do for free instead of paying for them, like going for a run instead of going to the gym. The lists would be endless, and it would be impossible to measure the volume of work done with any degree of accuracy.

Furthermore, how would we measure the value of work? How would cooking a meal at home compare to eating out? How does a run outside compare to a run on the treadmill in the gym, and does that answer change depending on where you run and what the weather is like at the time? The value of work done would be very arbitrary. So instead of desperately trying to measure the size of the natural economy in any meaningful way, there is perhaps a simpler, much more eloquent solution: Given that the value of the total economy can be measured by aggregating the natural and monetary economies, and we want to create a healthy balance between the monetary and natural economies, instead of ringing the alarm bells when GDP doesn't increase, ring them when it does increase.

In addition, there are a whole host of other metrics that we should consider as well to measure our success, such as air quality, water quality, global temperatures, biodiversity levels, and mental health issues, rather than letting a single metric dominate. It is frankly concerning that modern-day economics is motivated by endlessly growing something that is not directly tied to the welfare of the population. Surely, economic thinking today ought to concentrate on the issues that matter to individuals, which is only possible by growing a metric that does take into account the overall well-being of the people, rather than chasing relentless monetary growth.

As we (hopefully) shift away from the monetary economy and towards the natural economy, this will have implications for businesses, financial services, and governments. Businesses want to charge money for their services so they can make a profit, investors want a monetary return on their financial investment, and governments enact taxes to pay for services, which requires a monetary economy.

For all these reasons, there will be resistance to shrinking the monetary economy. However, we need to change our mindset, which today is fixated on monetary value. If employees and other stakeholders, such as customers and communities, own businesses instead of shareholders, then profit and monetary gain need not be the overriding objective for the business. It can even become an objective for the business to educate their customers to become less reliant on their services, shifting customer demand for their products and services to the natural economy, where people help themselves and their communities rather than buy from big businesses. For example, a clothes manufacturer offering advice on how to upcycle old clothes rather than selling new clothes, or a bakery giving away recipes and advice on how to bake your own bread. With less business, the clothes manufacturer and baker can reduce their working hours, meaning they now have time to do more things for *themselves* rather than purchasing goods and services from other companies.

The role of banks and other financial institutions will need to shift to helping businesses shrink their businesses in a controlled way. I would like to highlight that this is not an entirely alien idea, as they are *already* playing this role for distressed and failing businesses, but now they would need to do this for the majority of businesses. In fact, it should be an easier task, as it would be done in a controlled and planned manner, rather than as a result of an unplanned failure. The challenge for them will be to change their mindset as their own business also needs to shrink, including their profits.

And just as businesses shrink, the government services shrink too, as individuals and communities take on more of these services, rather than relying on the state to provide them. So, as the monetary economy shrinks, government revenue raised from taxes will shrink, and so too should government spending. As we travel less, the transport budget can shrink; as we get less sick, the healthcare budget can shrink; as we spend less, the pensions and welfare budgets can shrink; and so on. Of course, the welfare state will still be essential to help those who need it most, but in transitioning to a more sustainable lifestyle, it is intuitive that individuals will naturally rely on it less.

Overall, I hope that this chapter has demonstrated the dangers of letting the single metric of GDP dominate. Whilst it is undeniably a helpful tool to understand the monetary economy, it neglects to account for many other variables and hence is not a good proxy for the standard of living of the population today. Instead, we must find a balance between the monetary and natural economies, such that the overall contentment of society is maximised.

CHAPTER 8

UNINTENDED CONSEQUENCES

Before you strike a match or start a market: you
never know what riches it may reduce to ashes.
—Kate Raworth

In Raworth's second way to think like a twenty-first-century economist, she asks us to tell a new story, as the story we've been told is how free markets will create wealth, that the state should not interfere, as market forces will always drive out the best solution. Capitalists tell us that the marketplace will make everything better by finding solutions to the world's problems, but the reality is, they caused the problems in the first place. They will argue that either demand for greener products or regulations to help the environment will ensure entrepreneurs find solutions to the world's problems. Whilst to an extent this is true, along with each new invention usually comes unintended consequences which create more issues, and the examples we could use to illustrate this seem endless.

For example, the Industrial Revolution brought much prosperity, but it also meant air pollution. One thing we were encouraged to do to combat air pollution was to switch petrol cars for diesel, as it was thought to have less of an effect on air quality. However, it turns out that they have very tiny particles that are extremely bad for us, and in fact diesel cars create more pollution than petrol cars, so we switch back to petrol cars. Now we will aim to switch to electric cars, but do we really understand all the unintended consequences? For example, what's the impact of digging up seabeds to mine for the required minerals, or disposing of batteries when they become obsolete? Or will we ditch all of them and replace them with hydrogen cars?

When we put chlorofluorocarbons (CFCs) in fridges and aerosols, we had no idea that they would destroy the ozone layer. After we found out, we had to ban them.

LED lights have been hailed as a great invention, as they only use a fraction of the electricity compared to regular lights. However, there are now concerns that blue light emitted from LED lights at night may disturb our sleep patterns and increase our risk of developing diseases including cancer, diabetes, heart disease, and obesity.[26]

Adding fertilisers to the soil was introduced to give a greater yield to our crops. However, we now know that they harm the microbes in the soil, reduce soil fertility, and when washed into our streams and rivers, create excessive algae which depletes the oxygen in the water.

In Britain, when we started managing human-made plantations to grow timber, we got rid of the thorny scrubs that would surround the trees, as they got in the way and were seen as a hindrance. However, without the thorny scrubs to protect young saplings, grazing and browsing animals would cause devastation to them. As a result, livestock such as deer had to be kept out of the plantations by using fences or ditches around the borders. The book *Wilding* by Isabella Tree is littered with numerous examples of where humans try to give

---

[26] Harvard Medical School, https://www.health.harvard.edu/staying-healthy/blue-light-has-a-dark-side

nature a helping hand with our "We know best" philosophy; it doesn't go to plan, but where we just leave nature to do its own thing, we get spectacular results. Every time we go against nature, and forge ahead with our human-made inventions, or just intervene with nature, we have to be aware of the unintended consequences.

Mobile phones are a true archetype of this, as they enable us to do so many more things, but we there are huge drawbacks too. For example, chiropractors are reporting an increase in back problems in children as the positions they sit in with their phones are unnatural. Add in social media and artificial intelligence, and we can see both the benefits and problems of new technology growing at an exponential rate. Social media has brought us many benefits, such as reconnecting with lost friends, having relationships with people from all over the world, and raising awareness on important issues. However, the unintended consequences are vast: mental health issues, fake news, addiction, technical connection but physical isolation, changing the fabric of social society, cyber bullying, and Snapchat dysmorphia.

Today, there is so much fake news and misinformation that we can't even agree on what the truth is. Some people speculate about the potential for the future of artificial intelligence to take control over humans; this conjures up thoughts of a future like *The Terminator*, with violent machines and mass wars. However, the reality of the AI takeover is more subtle, and in fact the journey has already begun. Have you ever wondered why Facebook is valued at over half a trillion dollars, and yet you never pay to use it? The documentary *The Social Dilemma*,[27] created by highly ranked ex-employees of social media platforms, determined that the answer is that you are the product, and big businesses are paying to change your behaviour. It

[27] Netflix, *The Social Dilemma,* https://www.netflix.com/gb/title/81254224

is the job of Facebook and other social media companies to get you to spend as long as possible on their platform so they can learn more about you and influence your behaviour. The longer you spend on it, the more content they can put in front of you, and they choose what content you get to see. They use algorithms and machine learning to constantly improve their understanding of you and how they can best influence you, and they are getting better at it exponentially.

Remember, every dollar of the half a trillion-plus valuation is justified by their ability to change your behaviour to do what businesses want you to do. The AI takeover of humans has already started. Perhaps the most notable thing about the documentary was that it showed the very creators of social media, who had originally thought they created a force for good, turning on their own invention and essentially begging viewers to do the same. If we were to document all the examples of unintended consequences, it wouldn't just be a large book; it would fill a whole library. Even the best-intentioned human-made inventions, including those designed to reduce the harm we do to the environment, have unintended consequences; hopefully, these inventions will do more good than harm, but they may not be completely harm-free.

So whilst it is good to invest in new technologies such as renewable energy, to replace plastic packaging with biodegradable alternatives, to produce detergents which are less harmful to the environment, we cannot rely entirely on these new solutions, as some of them will inevitably come with a new set of problems. The bigger goal has to be to reduce demand for energy, for packaging, for detergents, and for goods and services in general. We need to contract rather than expand our monetary economies and return to a more natural way of life. Investment in green technologies should be seen as a way to help us reduce our environmental footprint whilst we transition to a more natural way of life, rather than an opportunity to grow our energy consumption and boost the world economies.

CHAPTER 9

A GREEN RECOVERY: PROCEED WITH CAUTION

The Green Party in the UK, and even other politicians, are calling for a Green Recovery following the economic downturn from Covid-19. This is a chance to replace some of the old economic activity that was destroying our planet with investment in renewable energies and other green technologies. Whilst such a recovery would be more beneficial than a recovery based on old industrial ways, we should be cautious about blindly overinvesting in new technologies where we don't fully understand the long-term effects. As previously discussed, there will be unintended consequences.

After World War II, a Green Revolution was hailed. The industrialisation of agriculture was deemed a green revolution, as Britain sought to grow more of its own produce. Artificial fertilisers were nothing short of a miracle, enabling enhanced yields of crops on ground not that suited to growing crops. Bigger machinery was used to bring economies of scale to the production process, and new varieties of crops were developed. To make way for all this new farming, hedgerows were ripped out at an alarming rate. Eventually, the government realised this was not a good thing and put in safeguarding measures, but even then, eighty thousand miles of hedgerows, enough to circle the world three times, vanished in the UK in the ten years after the safeguarding legislation.[28] Trees had no place in this new age of industrial agriculture, as they took up valuable growing space. Ancient oak trees were destroyed to make way for growing crops, something that seems inherently disrespectful and conspicuously bad for the environment.

Additionally, through the use of synthetic fertilisers, we have gained short-term boosts in productivity at the expense of long-term soil degradation. Unless we change, we will run out of arable soil within the next sixty years.[29] Furthermore, as we use fertilisers to increase our yields, the biodiversity in the soil decreases, and more fertiliser is needed to achieve the same yields. So here we are, caught in yet another vicious circle of self-destruction.

In hindsight, we can see that this so-called Green Revolution has left us with poor quality soil following the use of artificial fertilisers, not to mention the impact the fertilisers have had on the wildlife in our seas and rivers as it gets washed into them. The natural habitat for bees, butterflies, and other insects has been dramatically reduced as hedgerows have disappeared. And now we stand and judge Brazil for cutting down the Amazon rainforest to make way for grazing cattle and growing soya beans, as we know these ancient trees are the lungs of the planet, vital to its survival, even though we did the same thing to our own trees not long ago, albeit on a smaller scale.

---

[28] The Independent, 26 October 1996, https://www.independent.co.uk/news/uk/home-news/the-hedgerow-8000-miles-vanish-each-year-1360413.html

[29] *Scientific American,* https://www.scientificamerican.com/article/only-60-years-of-farming-left-if-soil-degradation-continues/

Looking back at history demonstrates the danger of jumping on the bandwagon of a green movement without entirely understanding what it means. What people refer to when they talk about the Green Economy isn't really clear, as it isn't really green. It's just less black than our current economy. That is not to say we should abandon these greener alternatives; they provide an attractive and immediate stepping stone away from fossil fuels to curb climate change and pollution in the short term. Indeed, I not only put solar panels on my roof, I have invested in start-up companies developing renewable energies including solar, wind, wave, and tidal power. However, we must recognise that the real Green Economy is the natural economy working with nature, living a more self-sufficient lifestyle. The bigger goal needs to be reducing total consumption. For example, let's say the environmental damage caused by fossil fuels is twice as much as renewable energies (I am not saying it is, it's probably much worse, but we don't yet know all the consequences of renewable energies). In twenty-five years' time, when we have totally replaced fossil fuels with renewable energy, if we have doubled energy consumption, then we are back to square one in terms of environmental impact.

CHAPTER 10

TERRORISM AND DEFENCE

We live in a world with vast disparities in wealth; there are multibillionaires who, on an average day, will increase their wealth by more than what most people will amass in a lifetime. At the other end of the spectrum, there are 689 million people (1 in 10 people worldwide) living on $1.90 or less per day.[30] The amount of money that the poorest people will earn over their entire lifetime may be less than what the richest few will earn during just one hour whilst they sleep. With such large disparities, it is no wonder there is discontent and resentment in the world, particularly towards Western societies.

As our technological journey progresses, there is no escape from the goods and services produced by large multinationals. Communities which hold different values to Western society can no longer escape from it; the wealth we have accumulated is clear for all to see, and the goods and services we sell are dangled in front of the whole globe and its children. A community which has been self-sufficient for centuries will find it difficult to turn away a large multinational

---

[30] World Bank, https://www.worldbank.org/en/topic/poverty/overview

who offers local investment to set up shop there, promising jobs and prosperity.

It is Western modern living that is destroying the planet. We take up far more than our fair share of the earth's resources (for example, if everyone in the world lived like the average person in the USA, five earths would be required to sustain our lifestyles[31]). Or to put it another way, the average US citizen consumes seven times more than the average citizen in India.

Most of what we consume is made abroad, so the environmental impact is effectively exported to locations often with little or no regulations. So not only are we responsible for putting the whole earth and the entire of humanity at risk, but in the pursuit of additional profit, we seek to expand our businesses to every corner of the planet, getting every community on it to buy into our Western goods, services, and values. A religious community might require women to dress conservatively, as they do not want men to view them as sexual beings, but now in today's global society, their children have access to hardcore pornography on the internet. And then when there is a terrorist attack on the West, we are surprised and shocked that there could be such evil people doing such things.

Whilst any attack on any other human being is innately a bad thing and certainly to be discouraged, we should take a look at exactly *why* this is happening. Although we are certainly advancing in our ability to combat terrorist attacks, there is no denying that the problem itself is not going away. Take the example of our approach to fighting cancer. We are getting very good at fighting cancer; we do lots of monitoring and screening to catch the cancer early, and then we have

---

[31] Science Alert, https://www.sciencealert.com/we-just-used-up-all-of-earth-s-resources-for-the-year-and-it-s-only-july

developed a huge range of drugs and treatments to kill the cancer off when it's detected. We have spent many billions on this very lucrative business, but if we take a step back, we can see that cancer rates are rising, and rather than just fighting the cancer as it appears, it would be better for all to prevent it in the first place.

Similarly, with terrorists, we have seen a growth in the number of attacks. We can use our intelligence networks to identify potential attacks, and we can use the police force, the armed services, and all their weaponry to fight it, and we have become good at that. But shouldn't we be asking the question, why do people want to attack us? It seems to me, that until we answer this question, no matter how much intelligence gathering or weaponry we acquire, there will continue to be people who wish to attack us.

We can look at the ideology of terrorists and quickly jump to conclusions that their values are wrong. However, with so many growing movements which seek to attack Western society and its values, we do need to accept that other people have other perspectives. Perhaps, if we had been born in a different country with a different culture, we could even think that way too.

I am by no means saying that I comprehend the motivations for terrorist attacks; however, I don't think we should be surprised that there is anger and resentment towards the West when we are destroying the planet; taking more than our fair share of the earth's resources; pushing our Western goods, services, and values on the rest of the globe; and generating such huge disparities between rich and poor.

The same applies to defence. The UK is currently spending £42.2bn per year on defence.[32] The purpose of this is to ensure that we are able

---

[32] Statista, https://www.statista.com/statistics/298490/defense-spending-united-kingdom-uk/

to defend ourselves against other nations who may attack us. Again, we need to ask ourselves the question as to why they would want to attack us. In addition to all the reasons outlined for terrorism, we should also look at the relative power nations have. It is a bit similar to a bully in the playground. For example, he may be the biggest and strongest character and have a gang of a few guys who fit in with his ideologies. Those whom they see as misfits, having a different ideology, or trying to challenge them in any way had better watch out. However, when people have such power, others don't like it and try to find ways to dispel their power.

If we think of the rich Western countries as the cool guys, and the USA as the ringleader, there are plenty of other countries that have different ideologies that we may think don't fit in. Imagine if you lived in one of those countries. You would very likely have a very different set of values than the ones you have developed by living in Western society. You would see the USA and its allies as having a lot more wealth and power than you. You would see large multinationals that operate out of those countries, selling their goods and services into your country, disrupting your culture, and imposing Western values. Furthermore, the USA and its allies don't trust your country, and despite their greater wealth, bigger armies, and more potent weaponry, they don't allow you to have the same weaponry, as they perceive that it would be dangerous. It very much seems like one rule for them because they know best, and another rule for everyone else.

Let's take a look at a country like Costa Rica. Costa Rica has no army, navy, or air force, no heavy weapons of any kind. Instead, they plough their resources into being environmentally friendly, such as ecotourism and renewable energies. Who is going to feel anger and resentment at such a country? Well, despite not having the same level of defence forces to combat or deter terrorism, there has been no history of terrorist attacks in the country.

Overall, I am not trying to say that if we simply transition away from the monetary economy, all forms of terrorism will disappear and there will be no need for any kind of defence spending. However, given that there are such a variety of distinct cultures across the globe, it is not surprising that we have different values that conflict from time to time. I think there is certainly something to be said for deep socio-economic inequality augmenting division in society, and driving groups with cultural differences violently against each other. By narrowing the wealth gap, it is only logical that societal division will lessen, which is likely to reduce terrorist attacks, and with a reduction in potential threats, the budget for defence spending can fall too. Like with our fight against cancer, we may stand a better chance of winning the fight against terrorism, and better defend our country, if we stop fighting the symptoms and begin addressing the root cause, whilst saving a few billion quid in the process.

CHAPTER 11

NATURE WILL ALWAYS PREVAIL

No matter how badly we treat our planet, Mother Earth will always survive and flourish in the long run. It's actually the human race, ourselves, that we need to be more concerned with. If we treat the earth so badly that it can no longer sustain human life, then we will get wiped out. But there will be elements of nature that will continue to survive, and gradually the earth will flourish and will be made beautiful again.

When the atomic bomb was dropped on Hiroshima, no human was able to withstand the explosion. Gingko trees, however, did survive and are still there to this day.

Another example of how amazing our planet is, is to discover what happens if we just leave it alone, as in the rewilding experiment carried out at Oostvaardersplassen in the Netherlands.[33] In essence, the project took an area of reclaimed land and simply allowed nature to take its course, without any human intervention. Animals that would have been native to the area were reintroduced to the reserve, and the rest was left to nature. The results were outstanding, as nature did its work, and biodiversity quickly flourished, beyond expectations. The

---

[33] Staatsbosbeheer, https://www.staatsbosbeheer.nl/

experiment faced some criticism, as some aspects were considered inhumane, such as allowing some cattle, ponies, and deer to die at the end of winter. However, the quality of their lives was much better; the animals were no longer cooped up in a factory, or pushed around by humans. Instead, they grazed naturally on what they are designed to eat rather than eating food fed to them by humans; they also had normal sex rather than being artificially inseminated. The biodiversity that resulted from them living a completely natural life was considerably richer, stimulating a much greater variety of animal and plant life than any seasonal farmland grazing. Furthermore, these dying animals give back to the land, completing the circle of life.

A similar wilding exercise took place at Knepp in West Sussex.[34] Knepp is a thirty-five hundred-acre estate that used to be intensively farmed, and then in 2001 Sir Charles Burrell, the land owner, took the decision to fence off the area to let nature take over. Using grazing animals as the drivers of habitat creation, and with the restoration of dynamic, natural water courses, the project has seen extraordinary increases in wildlife. Extremely rare species like turtle doves, nightingales, peregrine falcons, and purple emperor butterflies are now breeding there; and populations of more common species are rocketing. They found many striking differences in the animals now that they were left to their own devices rather than being farmed and managed by humans. With cows, for example, there were no more painful bacterial infections caused by overmilking them. The natural social dynamics of the herd were very different; they survived the winter without the need for humans to feed them, and then they gave birth to healthy calves without the need for vets. It seems that whenever we interfere with nature, no matter how good our intentions,

---

[34] Isabella Tree, *Wilding.*

we always create some unfortunate unintended consequence; we'd be better off just letting nature be nature.

We cannot fight nature. Nature is complex in galactic proportions. Nature is so interconnected that we will never fully understand it. With all our technological developments, we think we can outsmart nature, but we can't even come close. For example, think of the technology used to build a spacecraft and send people into space. We think it's pretty cool. However, compare this to any living plant or animal, and the complexity of the rocket suddenly seems quite basic by comparison. Imagine trying to write a program to replicate all the bodily functions of an animal: how they move, eat, think, make decisions, reproduce, and so on. There is so much about nature that we don't understand, but rather than trying to understand it and alter it, all we need to do is work with it and embrace it.

For example, there are billions of microbes in a teaspoon of soil; we know we are destroying the soil with our modern farming practices, but we don't even know what we are destroying. We thought we were smart by enhancing crop yields by using fertilisers, but the reality is that over time, we have massively depleted the nutritional value of what has been grown using fertilisers, and if we carry on in the same way, in a couple of generations, the soil quality will be so poor we will hardly be able to grow anything. Most technological developments take us one step further away from nature, and hence there are unintended consequences, which we then try to compensate for with yet more unnatural solutions. All biodiversity is joined up globally, and we are totally reliant on it; the more we destroy it or meddle with it, the more problems we will experience.

Here are a few of the many points raised in the BBC documentary *Extinction: The Facts*:[35]

- We are losing biodiversity at a rate which is unprecedented in human history.
- The single biggest driver of biodiversity loss is destruction of natural habitat. In future it will be climate change.
- We are losing insects which are food for others in the food chain and insects are also required for pollination.
- Mammals have disappeared by 60 per cent since 1970.
- There are 1 million species at risk of extinction. This extinction is at a rate 100 times faster than what it should be and that rate is increasing.
- We have completely destroyed the natural balance of marine life in the world's oceans.
- When we take away large animals from our environment then smaller animals thrive (e.g., rats) which are more likely to carry diseases.
- Climate change will threaten our ability to feed ourselves.
- Plastic levels in killer whales found in Scotland was the highest ever found. As a result, they can't reproduce and will die out in the UK.

Instead of perpetuating the vicious circles of economic growth, we need to harness the virtuous cycle of nature. As plants and animals

35 BBC, *Extinction: The Facts*, https://www.bbc.co.uk/programmes/m000mn4n

get old, they will die off, but not before they have reproduced, and the waste from dying plants and animals is recycled to produce the nutrients for more life to flourish. The cycle of life that nature provides us with is perfect. It is totally unlike the human-made world, where our products always inevitably need replacing, and the process to recycle them is so much less perfect.

CHAPTER 12

SOLUTIONS

I hope I have convinced you thus far of the plethora of problems caused by modern living, which may have left you feeling a little uneasy. But fear not, reader. For I have dedicated the rest of this book to providing some ideas as to how we can tackle these undesirable problems. So with these vicious circles of economic growth at play, how do we jump off the treadmill and go back to a more natural way of living? When you've got a family to support, a mortgage, and various other financial commitments, it's not that easy to just move to the countryside in pursuit of a more natural lifestyle. There are people who have done it, but it's too big a step for most, and we can't just all do it en masse; there would be chaos. We need a more controlled and gradual way to reduce our reliance on economic growth; we can adopt simple things that enable us to replace human-made goods and services with more natural living. Let's first explore how we can redistribute wealth from the ultra-rich few to the many, lightening the pressure for people to work harder to make ends meet. We can then look at how we can transition to a more natural way of living.

CHAPTER 13

TAXING MULTINATIONALS

We've discussed how wealth is becoming increasingly concentrated in a very small percentage of the richest people in the world. The wealth is generated by large multinational companies which the rich own and manage. These multinationals often pay very little corporate tax (i.e., tax on their profits). They are able to engage in something called tax avoidance. Unlike tax evasion, which is illegal, tax avoidance is absolutely legal. The multinationals can move profits around to ensure that they pay little or no tax in countries with high taxation, and have their profits taxed in low tax countries, or even offshore havens where the tax rate is zero.

It's only rational for companies to minimise their tax bills whilst staying on the right side of the law. We all do it, and the richer we get, the more opportunities there are to do it. For example, most people will put money into a pension; obviously, the idea is to save for old age, but the reason we choose to put it in a pension and not just another bank account or investment account is because we get tax relief on the contributions made. Those who have enough money to save or invest, choose to put our money in an ISA because it's tax-free. So just as we all seek to minimise our tax bills, we should expect multinationals to do the same. It is the way we tax multinationals that needs to change.

As the largest companies in the world are now truly global, operating in all the major economies of the planet, it has become increasingly easy for them to move profits from one country to another to avoid tax. Historically, companies would make most, if not all, of their profits in just one country. Taxing companies on the profits they made in that country therefore made sense. However, as the shift has been made from making profits on a national level to a global level, the tax system has not kept up, with each country setting its own corporate tax rates, which apply only to profits made in the country. Of course, the tax authorities around the globe are well aware of this, and complex tax treaties are put in place to attempt to ensure a fair distribution of taxation between countries, minimising both tax avoidance and double taxation. However, corporate tax is still only applied at a national level and has not kept pace with the transition of companies operating from a national level to a global level.

Let's first take a look at how the tax avoidance works. Multinationals make profits in many different countries. They run a group of companies operating in different countries. They may have a head office or holding company which owns other companies, called subsidiaries. These companies will trade with each other, and by varying the price at which goods and services move from one place to another (transfer pricing), they can move profits around. The head office could charge other companies for services, such as branding, reducing profits in its subsidiaries and increasing profits in the head office. So, as companies make profits in different countries, they can move profits to countries with the lowest tax rates. For example, many companies set up their head office in Ireland, where corporate taxes are low. Ireland makes big profits but pays low tax, while the other countries in which the company trades make little or no profit and so pay little or no taxes.

Transfer pricing moves profits to a low tax location

Government responses around the globe have been a race to the bottom in terms of corporate tax rates so that their country is more attractive than others, as getting a small percentage of something big is better than getting a large percentage of little or nothing.

Most countries used to charge businesses 50 per cent or more in tax, but now most charge 30 per cent or less. The clear winner has been Ireland, where corporate tax has been slashed from 50 to 12.5 per cent and as a result has managed to attract many businesses to set up their head office there. The chart on the next page shows how corporate tax rates have fallen:[36]

[36] Data sourced from https://tradingeconomics.com/

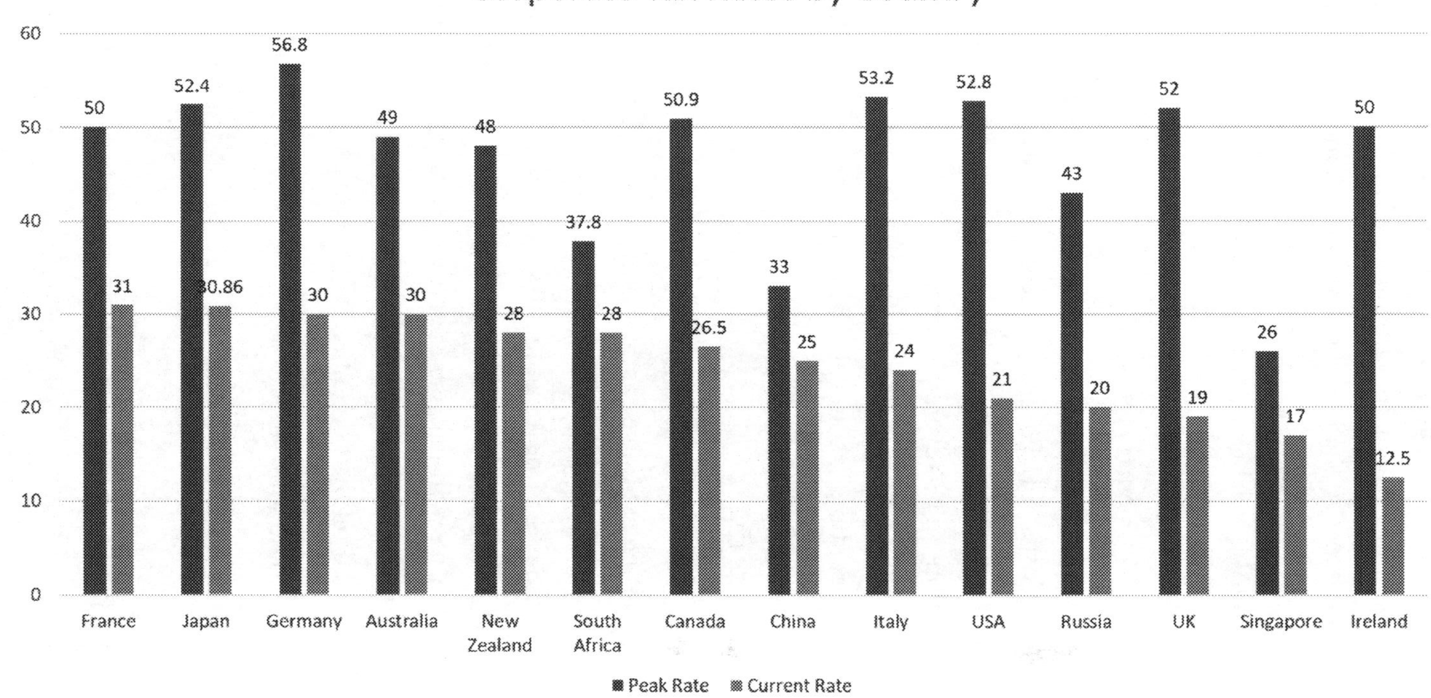

Source: Trading Economics, https://tradingeconomics.com/

Not only have corporate tax rates fallen dramatically, in the UK, we used to have one rate for small businesses and another for large businesses. But because the large businesses can move their profits, the higher rates for large businesses have been abolished in an attempt to attract them to do business in the UK.

The disproportionately low rates of tax paid by multinationals demonstrate that our current system for taxation, operating in the basis of national profits, is not working. Instead, we need to focus on the global profits for the group. Ideally, we would just apply a global tax to these companies, set by an international body, such as the United Nations. The revenue generated from the taxation could not only be used to distribute wealth from the super rich to the less well-off within a nation, it could also be used to transfer wealth from rich countries to poorer countries.

However, implementing such a global tax would require many countries to agree, and every country would have a different view on how it should be set up so that it would be most beneficial, or at least not too harmful, to their own country. Such a coordination effect could take decades and never amount to anything. So we have to implement something that can work unilaterally on a national level. One idea, which we will call Fair Share corporate tax, could be to target global profits but then moderate them to the respective country, for example, based on the percentage of sales made in that country.

So the formula could look like:

$$\textbf{Fair Share Tax} = \textbf{Global Profits} \times \textbf{Tax Rate} \times \frac{\textbf{National Sales}}{\textbf{Global Sales}}$$

"Sales" being the value of goods and services sold, whereas profit is sales minus costs. In terms of the tax rate, 50 per cent is a fair tax rate for large multinationals. They used to pay at least this much in most countries before they started shifting profits around to avoid tax.

Now let's look at some examples of some large multinationals: Facebook, Apple, Amazon, and Starbucks. They made vast revenues, yet paid very little tax in the UK over the past couple of years. The tax calculations for these companies in the UK would look like this:[37]

Year	Company	Global Sales		UK Sales	UK	Global Profits		Fair Share Tax	Actual Tax
		$m	£m	£m	Share	$m	£m	£m	£m
2018	Facebook	55,838	43,825	797	1.82%	25,361	19,905	181	28
	Apple	265,595	208,457	1,196	0.57%	72,903	57,219	164	6
	Amazon	232,887	176,296	2,959	1.68%	10,073	7,906	66	6
	Starbucks	24,720	18,713	388	2.07%	4,518	3,546	37	4
2019	Facebook	70,697	53,518	1,071	2.00%	23,986	18,157	182	29
	Apple	260,174	196,952	1,378	0.70%	65,737	49,763	174	4
	Amazon	280,522	212,356	2,256	1.06%	11,588	9,095	48	1
	Starbucks	26,509	20,067	362	1.80%	3,599	2,825	25	2

Their fair share tax would be between 6 and 48 times the actual tax they currently pay, on average more than 10 times the tax in both 2018 and 2019. They can afford it, as they in fact paid this much in the past.

---

[37] All figures taken from Facebook, Apple, Amazon, and Starbucks financial statements for the group and UK subsidiary (Facebook UK Limited, Apple Retail UK Limited, Amazon UK Services Limited, and Starbucks Coffee Company UK Limited). Group numbers have been converted from USD to GBP at the year-end spot rates of 1.2741 (31st Dec 2018) and 1.321 (31st Dec 2019). Note Starbucks Coffee Company (UK) Limited has a financial year end of 30 September, which has been used to align to the Starbucks group accounts, which have a year-end of 31 December. All other group companies and associated subsidiary accounts have a financial year end of 31 December.

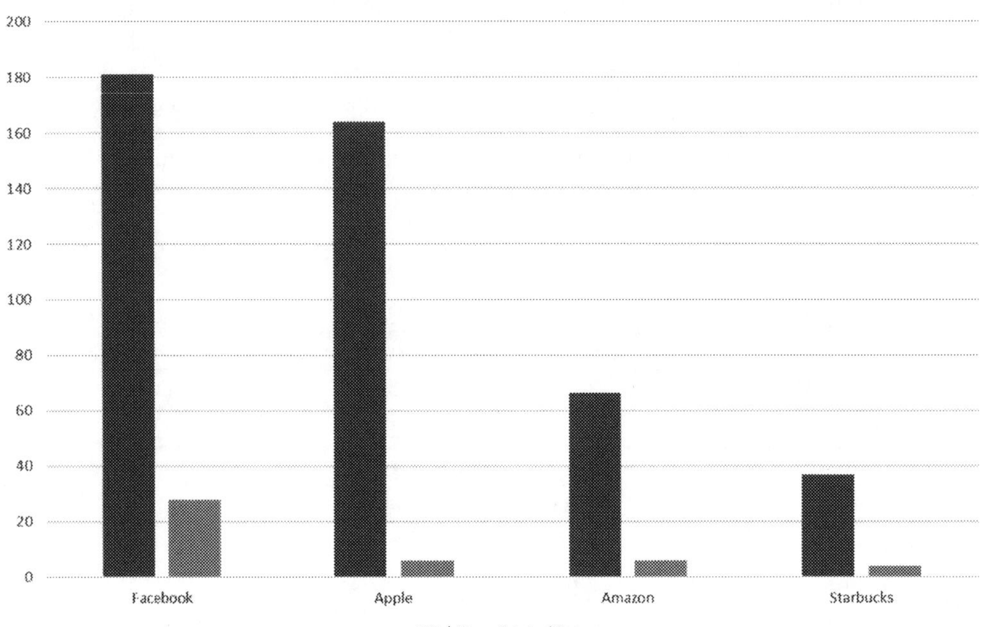
2018 Fair Tax Calculation v Actual Tax Paid
200
180
160
140
120
100
80
60
40
20
0
Facebook
Apple
Amazon
Starbucks
Fair Tax
Actual Tax

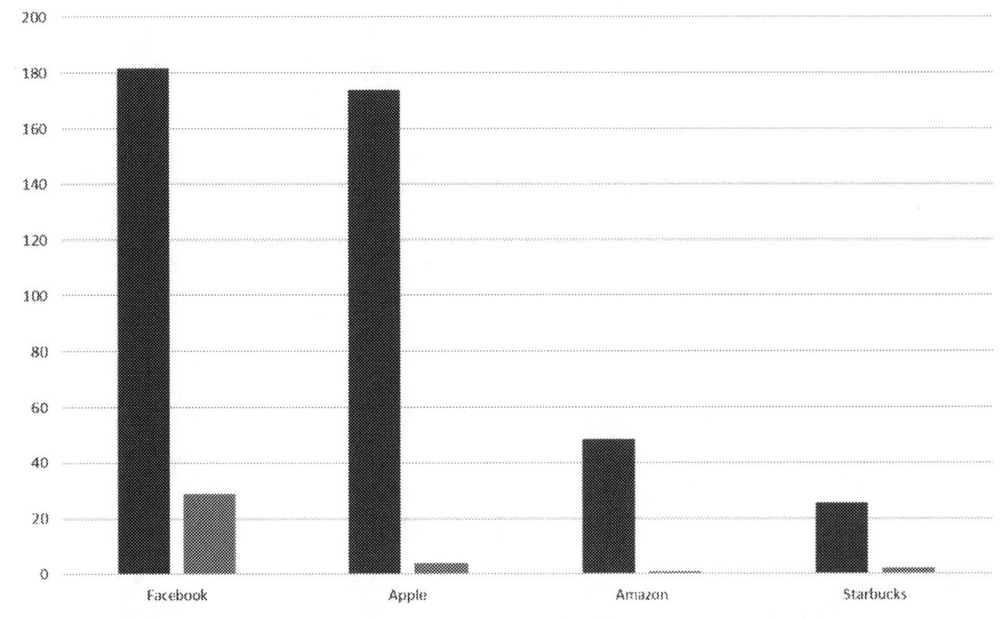
2019 Fair Tax Calculation v Actual Tax Paid
200
180
160
140
120
100
80
60
40
20
0
Facebook
Apple
Amazon
Starbucks
Fair Tax
Actual Tax

With such a high tax bill in the UK, would companies shun Britain as a place to do business? No; in fact, the UK would become a more attractive place for businesses. As with the current framework, countries that tax national profits incentivise companies to move profits away from these countries to reduce their tax bill. However, those countries which remove national profits from the equation incentivise businesses to set up their head office in their country and make big national profits.

To explain this, let's take an extreme example: If Apple were to have made all of their £57.7bn profit in 2018 in the UK, and exactly zero profit in every other country, then their UK tax bill would still be £164m. Apple would then avoid paying tax in other countries, unless they adopted the new formula, giving them an effective global rate of tax of just 0.3 per cent. Now the idea isn't to help companies to avoid tax in other countries; instead, the aim is for all countries to adopt this formula. If all countries adopted this method, then the global tax Apple would pay would be $36.5bn instead of the $13.4bn they actually paid. There is, however, a first adopter advantage, as if you have adopted the formula whilst other countries have not, then businesses will be attracted to your country despite the higher national tax bill.

The reason this formula is so vitally important is that it has the potential to drastically change where the current burden of tax falls. In the UK, a large multinational will pay just 19 per cent tax on profits. Contrast this with a worker on minimum wage who pays 20 per cent income tax and 12 per cent national insurance, so a marginal rate of 32 per cent tax on income. So the worker on minimum wage is paying a rate of tax that is two-thirds higher than what a large multinational pays on its profits, and that's before the multinational moves its profits overseas to avoid tax.

I would like to clarify that this new formula is not for small businesses, where profits are mainly generated in one country. Smaller businesses don't usually make excessive profits and therefore don't need to be taxed at such a high rate. But for the large multinationals generating extreme wealth for its owners, such a policy is necessary to rebalance the widening gap between rich and poor.

A paper Taxing Multinationals: A New Approach[38] outlines such an approach in detail. Their formula is more comprehensive, taking into account labour and capital as well as sales to apportion profits to a country. This more elaborate formula will give a more accurate apportionment of profit to a country, and will need to vary by industry. However, the fair tax calculations above which have been based on sales alone for simplicity would be representative of the more complex formula as the technology companies have a low labour and capital component and a high sales component. Such a formula will make it extremely difficult and impractical for companies to move their taxable profits to low tax countries.

In the 2019 election, the Labour party picked up on this paper and included the policy in their manifesto. However, it didn't get much publicity. Instead, the press focused more on the proposed increase in the corporation tax rate to 26 per cent, which was reported by critics as being anti-business. Perhaps what the Labour party failed to do, was to explain that irrespective of whether the tax rate was 19 per cent, 26 per cent or 50 per cent, the new formula would make the UK

---

[38] Public Services International, Taxing Multinationals: A New Approach https://pop-umbrella.s3.amazonaws.com/uploads/1acfb317-6e5a-4273-b950-57b3ed085d6b_Taxing_Multinationals_PSI.pdf

a tax haven as moving profits to the UK would not increase the UK tax bill but would reduce their global tax bill.

Some may challenge as to whether taking a unilateral approach to taxing global profits breaks international tax treaties. If they do, then worst case is these treaties need to be either torn up or re-written. Undoubtedly, there will be some resistance and challenges in implementing such a dramatic change to the way in which multinationals are taxed, not least of all from the multinationals themselves, who would lobby the government very hard. However, the current methodology, which sees all countries competing with one another to be the lowest tax country to attract businesses, cannot continue for long. Even many billionaires agree that their wealth should be taxed and distributed more evenly. Most will engage in philanthropy, giving back to their communities, tackling issues they feel most strongly about. However, none of them offer to top up their tax bill. Like the rest of us, they don't want to pay a penny more in tax than they have to.

The problem with introducing a new tax like this, which raises tax from companies which are headquartered elsewhere, is that there is a backlash from the country where they are headquartered. In this case, however, the aim is not to create tension with other countries, but rather it is to create unity, by asking them to adopt the same policy so that all countries get to increase their tax revenues. It's a winning strategy for every government; the only losers are the large multinationals.

Perhaps if most major countries did adopt such an approach, then the multinationals may even be supportive of abandoning a national corporate tax in favour of a global tax (e.g., operated by the United Nations at a flat rate of 50 per cent) that would enable the tax revenue to be distributed internationally, giving developing countries a boost to their incomes. It wouldn't materially impact the total tax the corporations pay, but as the developing countries become richer, this gives new opportunities for the multinationals to sell their products to a much wider market, as people in the now developed countries will be able to spend more.

Not to mention the tangible benefits to developing countries of having a much larger budget to be able to feed, clothe, and care for their populations. Now this may be getting ten steps ahead; it would be monumental if we just start to change the focus of how we tax multinationals. However, I hope this kick-starts the debate on how to become much bolder in terms of an appropriate tax rate and much more global in terms of the taxation approach for the companies which command a market capitalisation of many billions, despite being only a few years old.

An alternative approach has been proposed by the Independent Commission for the Reform of International Corporation Tax (ICRICT), whereby a US company would pay a minimum tax on its foreign earnings.[39] They give this example: "Imagine that Apple books $10 billion in profits in Ireland—taxed in Ireland at 5 percent—and $3 billion in Jersey—taxed in Jersey at 0 percent. The United States would tax Apple's Irish income at 16 percent and Apple's Jersey income at 21 percent. More broadly, the United States would impose country-by-country taxes so that Apple's effective tax rate, in each of the countries where it operates, equals at least 21 percent." Such an approach would remove the incentive for companies to shift

---

[39] Independent Commission for the Reform of International Corporate Taxation, https://www.icrict.com/you-should-also-read/2020/9/24/ending-corporate-tax-avoidance-and-tax-competition-a-plan-to-collect-the-tax-deficit-of-multinationals1

profits to low tax jurisdictions and encourage countries to increase their corporate taxes. They estimate that this would generate over $60bn in additional tax revenues, and that's just using a rate of 21 per cent for US companies. Imagine if all multinationals paid a rate of 50 per cent in all countries.

There are definitely viable solutions to reverse the race to the bottom of corporate tax that we have seen over the last few decades and get multinationals to pay their fair share. It doesn't even require international co-operation. It just requires the political will to do so, and just one bold country to take the lead.

CHAPTER 14

GLOBAL TAXATION

Whilst it may be difficult to levy taxation on corporations on a global level, it should be possible to get agreement to levy taxes at a government or country level to combat environmental issues like climate change. Take, for example, the Paris agreement; in 2016, fifty-five countries signed up to keep global temperatures from rising this century well below 2 degrees Celsius above pre-industrial levels and to pursue efforts to limit the temperature increase even further to 1.5 degrees Celsius. Nearly two hundred countries have now signed up to this.[40]

If they can reach agreement on this, then why not agree to impose a tax on each country depending on how much damage they are doing to the environment, for example, on the various greenhouse gas emissions made by the country? This would provide a much greater incentive to reduce emissions (or whatever the tax is levied on) than the Paris agreement does, which just takes a stock take every five years to assess collective global progress. If we start with just the G20 countries and levy a tax equivalent to around 1 or 2 per cent of

---

40 United Nations, https://unfccc.int/process/the-paris-agreement/status-of-ratification

their GDP, this could raise a trillion dollars or more, giving a massive incentive for countries to actually reduce their emissions. It would then be up to each country to work out how it raises the taxes in order to pay for it.

Raising a trillion dollars or more every year could then be put to good use to help developing countries invest in things like renewable energy. As we discussed in chapter 7, "The Natural Economy," developing countries still need to increase their GDP, bringing many people out of poverty to afford some of the basic things that we take for granted in the Western world, like access to clean drinking water, basic housing, and three meals a day. As the GDP of these countries increases, there is a real risk that their carbon footprint and environmental impact will increase. For them, the quickest way to get out of poverty may be to use the old technologies which have caused so much damage to the environment in the West (as, for example, petrol cars are cheaper than electric cars). A sizeable fund made available to invest in green technologies could go a long way to ensuring that they don't make the same disastrous mistakes as we did in developed countries, by causing such grave damage to the environment as we grew our economies. It's a win-win situation, as everyone will benefit from their reduced environmental impact, particularly with respect to climate change.

CHAPTER 15

SIN TAXES

Sin taxes, that is taxing goods and services which are deemed to have a harmful impact on individuals, communities or the environment, is something else that could raise substantial tax revenues as well as changing consumer behaviour for the better. We already have such sin taxes for goods such as cigarettes, alcohol and fuel. Some of these duties have been raised many times and as a result the price of the goods is substantially higher. For example, the price of cigarettes is about 5 times higher as a result of duty and VAT taxes,[41] and the price of petrol is about 3 times higher as a result of duty and VAT taxes.[42]

Imagine if the price of taking a flight tripled. There is no tax on the fuel used for flights, not even VAT! Why should this be the case if planes pollute the air just as much as cars? It's a bit more complicated, as planes can refuel in different countries, and there are international treaties on fuel tax, but ultimately there is no rationality behind taxing

---

[41] On average, 82 per cent of the retail price of cigarettes is tax, according to the Tobacco Manufacturers Association, http://the-tma.org.uk/policy-legislation/taxation/

[42] RAC Foundation, https://www.racfoundation.org/data/taxation-as-percentage-of-pump-price-data-page

fuel for cars and not fuel for planes. Alternatives such as a frequent flyer levy have been proposed (but not implemented). This may be a better way to implement such a tax, but the proposals are for very low rates of tax, as increasing the cost of flights substantially would be unpopular. Whilst the duty on petrol was increased gradually over many years, so that the price didn't triple overnight, we need now to be a bit more aggressive given how short a time frame we have before a climate change catastrophe. We have been given ten years by scientists (see more on this in chapter 20, "Tipping Point"), so we need to start making real changes now. If the price of a flight even doubled, or increased by 50 per cent, then people would start making substantially fewer fights, which is what needs to happen.

Now imagine if the price of processed red meat tripled. According to the WHO, eating processed red meat can cause cancer,[43] so it's not good for us. Add to this the environmental impact of farming for meat. For example, not only is cattle farming in itself contributing massively to climate change, as the demand for it is so high, but we are cutting down rainforests to make way for more cattle farming. In the UK, we can't really complain about the deforestation that goes on in the Amazon rainforest if we continue to contribute to the high level of demand for beef. According to Carbon Brief, "avoiding meat and dairy products is the single biggest way to reduce your environmental impact on the planet."[44]

---

[43] World Health Organization https://www.who.int/news-room/q-a-detail/q-a-on-the-carcinogenicity-of-the-consumption-of-red-meat-and-processed-meat

[44] Carbon Brief daily briefing, 1st June 2018 https://www.carbonbrief.org/daily-brief/avoiding-meat-and-dairy-is-single-biggest-way-to-reduce-your-impact-on-earth

There are many things we could tax, for example:

- single-use plastics
- detergents and chemicals, which pollute our rivers
- pesticides, which damage our health and the soil
- fertilisers, which are destroying wildlife in rivers and oceans
- meat and dairy, which contribute very heavily to greenhouse gasses and water shortages
- fish that are not sustainably caught
- food that is not from sustainable sources, such as non-sustainable palm oil and soya
- highly processed foods and fast foods, which are making us sick
- gas we burn to heat our homes
- electricity from non-sustainable energy
- aviation travel, which has a massive carbon footprint

As with the tax on petrol and cigarettes, we need to drastically increase the price of other sinful goods and services if we are to have a meaningful shift in people's behaviour. The increase could be done in phases to allow businesses and individuals to adapt, but it needs to be done, and it needs to be done quickly.

So why not hike the price of meat and dairy immediately? By heavily taxing meat and dairy, we can transition to a mainly plant-based diet. This will not only reduce the methane gasses that are released into the atmosphere from the livestock, but will free up lots of land as we need much less to produce plant-based food. The land can be rewilded, with trees planted to lock up carbon dioxide and enable biodiversity to flourish. There is an additional side effect of eating a mainly plant-based diet: We get healthier, as long as we avoid processed foods. Research has shown that switching away from meat and dairy products and towards a plant-based diet can result in a reduced risk of heart disease, strokes, and type 2 diabetes, as well as lowering blood pressure, reducing blood cholesterol, and promoting a healthy body weight.[45] We need to make this happen with immediate effect if we are to avoid a climate change catastrophe, as explained in chapter 20, "Tipping Point."

We could even just tax stuff in general. We produce so much stuff, most of which eventually ends up in landfill; some may take a few days to get there, others take many years. The tax would serve as a pre-payment on taking the product to landfill. If you resell the product, then the price you get for it would be inflated, as the second consumer would be willing to pay more as they don't directly pay the tax as a second-hand good, so there is an incentive to resell so it can continue to be used rather than taken to landfill. If we imposed a hefty tax on packaging, companies would be encouraged to use less of it to keep their prices down. Perhaps they would even aim to remove packaging altogether by using reusable containers, thereby avoiding the tax on every trip to the supermarket. For bigger ticket items, like white goods and mobile phones, if you sell it to a company that can reuse the components, that firm could claim back some or all of the tax, depending on how much they can reuse. This would even encourage manufacturers to make sure the parts can be reused to increase the resale prices.

Furthermore, if we use these taxes to fund a universal income (more on this in the next chapter), then the average person will not be out of pocket. Overall, it would be a zero-sum game. The average person would be no better or worse off. If you are more environmentally friendly than average, you would be better off, and if you are less

---

45 British Nutrition Foundation, https://www.nutrition.org.uk/healthyliving/helpingyoueatwell/plant-based-diets.html?start=1

environmentally friendly than average, you would be worse off. And if the taxes raised from the increased taxes on multinational profits are also used to fund a universal income, then despite the dramatic price hikes, everyone will be better off, and everyone will be incentivised to be more environmentally friendly.

For instance, say you had a disposable income of a hundred pounds a week to spend on food. After food sin taxes are added, you get a universal income of a hundred pounds, so you now have two hundred pounds to spend on food.

Food	Price before Tax	Tax	Price after Tax
Fresh Fruit and Vegetables	£25	0%	£25
Whole Grains and Pulses	£25	0%	£25
Meat and Dairy	£25	200%	£75
Processed Foods	£25	200%	£75
Total	£100		£200

You can see that if you don't change your spending habits, you are no better or worse off, but if you switch to a healthier, more sustainable diet, then you will be better off. Obviously, if lots of people switch to the healthier diet, then the universal income will fall as less taxes are raised, but the goal of changing behaviour has been achieved.

There are a couple of other potential sin taxes that are worthy of discussion. Firstly, illegal recreational drugs are currently tax free. You don't even pay VAT on them. And the vast profits made by drug dealers are also tax free. Making drugs legal would raise billions of pounds for the treasury. Of course, we need to put controls in place to ensure that drug use doesn't rise, but the current system is clearly not working. Every year, around 10 per cent of sixteen- to fifty-nine-year-olds will take illegal drugs in the UK,[46] so that's around 4 million people committing a crime every year. The police have been trying to prevent the supply of drugs in the UK for many decades, and yet more than 4 million people are able to get access to drugs. In fact, as my children tell me, when you are under the age of eighteen, it's easier to get hold of drugs than alcohol, because for alcohol, you need ID to prove your age. Drug dealers tend not to ask for any form of ID. The same policy of trying to control the supply of drugs by making them illegal continues year after year, without much success at all. Whilst they do catch and prosecute some dealers, others just take their place.

As it's not working, wouldn't it be better to at least consider an alternative approach? If all drug sales were nationalised, regulated and perhaps sold by trained social workers instead of dodgy dealers, then we could clean up and control the supply side of drugs. With drugs being illegal, the social and financial cost of supplying drugs is extremely high. At the start of the supply chain, farmers in third world countries put themselves and their families at risk by growing crops to try and keep their heads above water financially.

Then there is a huge number of people, some of whom are innocent bystanders who get in the way, government officials, or police officers, who get badly injured or murdered as drug dealers defend their territory against rival dealers and law enforcement officers. The deaths and violence occur both in the country producing the drugs and the country consuming them; this human cost is very high. From a financial perspective, drug dealers have high costs of buying

[46] European Monitoring Centre for Drugs and Drug Addiction, https://www.emcdda.europa.eu/countries/drug-reports/2019/united-kingdom/drug-use_en

weapons and security. All these deaths, violence, and costs would likely not occur if drugs were legal.

If the supply chain was managed by the government, not only would they make vast profits that could be put to better use for the good of its citizens, but the supply can be much better controlled. If 4 million people are going to take drugs on a regular basis, then isn't it better that they know exactly what they are buying, with a government health warning on the packet, and ID required to buy them? The drugs they buy today could be laced with other harmful substances, and there is no indication of what strength they are. The dealers don't care how old you are or what your circumstances are. If you purchased them from a trained professional instead, they could offer advice on how to give up or cut down. Their objectives would be to minimise sales, not maximise them, like drug dealers or companies. Cigarettes and tobacco could be controlled in the same way, taking the profits and motivation for sales away from large corporations.

A similar drugs policy already exists in the Green Party manifesto, but for some reason, there is little or no debate on the topic. Instead, the debate seems to be around decriminalising cannabis, which is an admission that the current policy wastes an awful lot of police resources but doesn't really address the wider issues. We should be asking the question, if you have a son or daughter, would you rather drugs be sold by a trained professional who will ID them and give them advice, including clear labelling of what they are taking, what strength they are, and the risks involved, or a drug dealer whose only advice will be "This is really good shit," but in reality, even they themselves have no idea what's in the packet they are selling. Perhaps a counterargument for making recreational drugs legal is that they will become more available or attractive to consumers. However, with vendors focussed on minimising sales and discouraging people from buying them, it would be the lesser of the two evils.

Another sin tax worthy of discussion, although "sin" is probably not the best way to refer to it, is population growth. The problem is, humans have taken over the world, and our lifestyles are consuming too much of the earth's resources. Today, we use the equivalent of 1.6 earths to provide the resources we use and absorb our waste. In other words it now takes the earth one year and eight months to regenerate what we use in a year.[47] Consequently, as the population grows, the problem gets even worse; this is one reason we are on course for a climate change disaster. Having a large family shouldn't be a sin, in my opinion, but given we are in such a critical point in history and in an attempt to avoid a massive catastrophe, we should consider measures to limit population growth.

To keep the population stable, we would need to average no more than two children per couple. Obviously, some have none or one, so some could have more, but the average would need to be two or less to avoid further population growth. It was encouraging to see Harry and Megan announce they would have no more than two children so they can preserve our planet for future generations. I've also met people who say they are choosing not to have any children because there are already too many people in the world, and having children will only accelerate climate change. Whilst true, it made me very sad that some people are forgoing the joy of having children out of concern for climate change. It may be worth considering a tax on larger families to reinforce the message that we need to limit population growth

---

[47] Global Footprint Network: Ecological Footprint, https://www.footprintnetwork.org/our-work/ecological-footprint/#:~:text=World%20Footprint,use%20and%20absorb%20our%20waste.

(even a very small tax). If we had a universal income (see chapter 16) then it could be a reduction in the universal income instead of a tax. If the purpose of the tax or reduction in benefit is clear, then most people will do the responsible thing and limit their family size. Perhaps others may feel they can have children as long as they limit it to one or two. I would very much hope this would be a temporary tax, and that future generations will be able to enjoy a healthy planet with whatever family size they choose.

Alternatively, if the taxation policies to share the wealth become truly global, then this could end population growth. Whilst it's the population in developed countries that are consuming most of the earth's resources, it's the developing countries who are driving the population growth. As they move out of poverty, their population will stabilise, as it has done in developing countries. By distributing wealth to those countries who have extreme poverty, we can stabilise the world population.

I appreciate that to introduce sin taxes at such high rates in such a short space of time may have some unintended consequences; thought needs to go into exactly what gets taxed and by how much. For example, we could heavily tax meat and dairy to reduce the environmental impact and improve our health, but not all meat has the same impact on the environment or our health. If livestock are raised on a natural pasture-fed diet (like they would if they were wild animals), there is much less harm to the environment; there are fewer health problems for both the animals and the humans who consume their meat and dairy. These were the findings in the Knepp farm wilding program.[48] So some thought is needed on exactly what gets taxed, but given the urgency of the situation we are in, it's also

---

[48] Isabella Tree, *Wilding.*

better to get this 80 per cent right than to not do anything about it, and refine the system over time.

Whilst I'm in favour of sin taxes to discourage the consumption of things which harm the planet, I'm less keen on incentives to encourage good behaviour. Often, what can happen is that the incentives become the sole reason for people changing their spending behaviour, rather than doing it for moral and social reasons. As a result, the behaviour will only continue if the incentives keep getting paid, which may not be sustainable. With sin taxes, it's easier to sustain a tax long term, as it's raising rather than spending money for the government. So, with the income raised from sin taxes, rather than subsidising environmentally friendly goods and services, I'm more in favour of spending it on a universal income.

CHAPTER 16

UNIVERSAL INCOME

A universal income is money the government would pay to all of its citizens that would be provided at the same level, irrespective of their income levels. This could even include a payment to children. This is necessary on many fronts. First and foremost, this will enable the vicious circles of economic growth to be broken. No longer will the majority of the population be caught in a trap where they are forced to both consume more and earn more. With the universal income, this will enable us to reduce the hours we work and still afford the rent. Those who choose to can then spend some of their free time pursuing a more natural way and self-sufficient way of life. For example, spending the time to grow fruit and vegetables at home or on an allotment will reduce economic activity, reduce your carbon footprint, save you money, and enhance your health (and hopefully happiness).

A universal income is very easy to administer. In the UK, various benefits in the welfare state have just been replaced with a universal credit system, designed to make things easier. However, it cost several billion pounds to roll out, is hugely expensive to administer, a few people will abuse it with fraudulent claims, and it has had numerous problems with many not able to access the benefits they deserve.

When you start earning, you effectively pay a marginal tax rate of 63 per cent as they reduce your universal credit (i.e., for every extra pound you earn, you will only be 37p better off). This is much higher than the top rate of income tax of 45 per cent and more than triple the 19 per cent corporate tax rate that large multinationals pay on their profits (that's if they leave any profits in the UK to be taxed). A universal income is not just cheap and easy to administer, but there is also no penalty for getting a job.

A universal income could be viewed as an income for all the unpaid work we do in the natural economy. Looking after children, doing household chores, and so on can be seen as just as valuable as paid work, enabling people to contribute to society in other, often more environmentally friendly ways, without the stigma associated with those not in paid employment.

With some of the universal income being funded from sin taxes, by avoiding those sin goods and services, you are effectively giving yourself a pay rise; you get to keep the taxes raised as other people spend their money on them, but you don't have to pay all the taxes, as you choose to spend your money on other, more environmentally friendly things. So you effectively get paid just for being an environmentally friendly citizen.

Ideally, a universal income would be global, so it would be truly universal. What you receive should not be defined by what borders you were born within. However, it will clearly be easier to implement on a national basis initially. If we ever get to implement some kind of global taxation (as we discussed in chapter 14, "Global Taxation"), then this would provide an ideal mechanism to facilitate a global universal income.

CHAPTER 17

REDISTRIBUTING WEALTH

So far, we have talked about taxing and redistributing income. However, the inequalities in accumulated wealth can be even more vast and also need to be addressed. It can be trickier to implement, as some people may be asset rich (e.g., owning property) but cash poor and hence don't have the funds to pay the taxes. Three European countries have a wealth tax, taxing a percentage of net worth above a certain level. However, they don't bring in a huge amount of tax (Switzerland being the most successful, where the wealth tax contributes around 3 per cent of taxes raised); there used to be many more European countries with wealth taxes, but most abandoned them, as they were hard to administer.

We need better ways in which we can redistribute wealth to reduce the growing inequalities. One idea could be to set up a global tax on billionaires, rather than a country-specific tax. According to Forbes,[49] there are 2,095 billionaires, so it is relatively easy to track them down and administer the tax. They have a net worth of $8 trillion, so a 1 per cent tax would raise $80 billion, or a 2 per cent tax $160 billion, not massive on a global scale, but a 1.5 per cent tax would be enough to give

---

49 Forbes, https://www.forbes.com/billionaires/

the 689 million people who live on $1.90 a day or less an extra 50c a day (a 25 per cent or more increase in income for them). This idea is far from the redistribution of wealth proposed by diehard-Marxists, trying to cap the idea of billionaires altogether, but it would have a significant impact on the poorest group in society without the same scale of resistance.

Another possibility is to move away from the concept of individual ownership of such assets, towards more community-based ownership. The two biggest stores of wealth to target are ownership of companies and ownership of land and property. In the case of companies, employees and other stakeholders could take ownership and receive the benefit of dividends, whilst investors could continue to supply debt funding, earning interest rather than profits. Of course, a transition from individual ownership to community ownership would be met with a great deal of resistance, but if the system of individual ownership is not fit for purpose, we should take a good look at how it can be made to work for the many and not just for the few.

One suggestion to achieve this for company ownership is to require companies to issue additional shares. For example, all companies greater than a certain size could issue say 1 per cent of investors share capital to employees, 1 per cent to customers, and 1 per cent to the local council. Unlike the shares held by employees, customers, and councils, the shares would not be tradable (bought and sold), but they would have the same entitlement to dividends and voting. As people cease to be employees or customers, they lose their share ownership, just as new employees and customers would immediately benefit from share ownership. As the new shares are issued, no money changes hands, and hence all companies can afford it.

Instead, the investors would see a dilution of their shares holding, and so they would suffer a reduction in value; this is effectively wealth tax applied to share holdings. At 3 per cent a year, after thirty-three years, the company would be owned equally between investors and other stakeholders. After a hundred years (if the scheme kept going that long and the world hasn't collapsed from climate change), then investors, employees, customers, and local councils would own a quarter of the company each. Any new capital injections that the company needs would be financed via debt, receiving interest instead of dividends. The governance of companies could then take a more holistic approach, balancing the needs of different stakeholders.

Clearly, a lot of thought would need to go into setting up such structures. For example, some companies don't have contact details for all their customers, or their customers may change from day to day or month to month. However, there will be solutions; it's not so different from running a loyalty card scheme, except instead of loyalty points, you get voting rights and a share of profits. Other stakeholders, such as suppliers, may be more worthy of a portion of the business. So, whilst a workable solution is not documented here, I hope the ideas can generate debate on what alternatives there may be to the current structure, where investors own 100 per cent of companies.

In the case of land, it could be owned by the community, with allocations made to families based on their need. We would no longer be a slave to the workplace to fund expensive mortgages or rent payments. Unlike companies, where you can give away a fraction of the corporation, it's not so easy with houses, so I am not suggesting people start giving up their own houses to the community. However, as new land is made available to property developers, perhaps we should look at alternatives, including making land available for more self-sufficient living. More on this in the next chapter.

CHAPTER 18

KIN DOMAINS

In *The Ringing Cedars of Russia* series of books, Anastasia outlines her vision for the future, of how we should transition from our current lifestyles to a more natural one. I will leave the detail to those books, but in summary, her vision has a hectare (or more) of land dedicated to each family, who live off the land. These family homesteads, or kin domains, would be in settlements of between one hundred and fifty and three hundred homesteads to form communities. After lobbying the government in Russia, Vladimir Megre was successful in getting a law passed such that anyone who wants such as family homestead will be given a hectare of land for just this purpose. As a result, there are hundreds of settlements that are popping up all over Russia, as families in pursuit of a more natural lifestyle take advantage of this new law. Over the past few years, many families have taken up this unique opportunity, with some very positive experiences documented on Megre's website.

Megre's website has articles and stories from people who have set up their own kin domain. Here is an extract from Elizaveta Krestyeva, who set up her own kin domain:[50]

> If you ask me, what question is most often asked to the settlers of the kin domains, including us, I will answer without hesitation:
>
> What do you live on?
>
> Options: how do you earn, is there a job, how much does it takes to live like this, and even build.?
>
> Probably 99 people out of a hundred ask about this, and only about this, in different ways. Sometimes for hours the conversation is spinning only around earnings. It drives me crazy.
>
> And very rarely someone asks the right question:
>
> How did you do it? How did you manage to create your kin domain? What needs to be done for this? How to start?
>
> And, unfortunately, my statistics show that people who are endlessly asking what to live on have practically no chance of creating their own kin domain.
>
> Because they live in a survival pattern where the main criterion is making money. And not even earning in the name of some goal, but simply making money, because as soon as this process stops, they will face a terrible death by starvation.
>
> They cannot prove that money is not a goal or even a means, but just an attribute that accompanies any movement towards a goal. You just have to have a goal, well, at least a lousy one!

---

[50] Vladimir Megre, https://vmegre.com/en/events/40592/

> Because money and opportunities come only for the purpose, and from multiple, sometimes the most unexpected sources, among which there may not be the usual official work at all.
>
> But people don't even understand what this is about. Their victim mentality dominates, for which over the past hundred years we have been well trained....
>
> And it is the guarantee that a person will never become the creator of his life and destiny. And the victims will carefully teach their children the same thinking.
>
> But you just need to change the question. People, not what, but how. Always remember, not what, but how!
>
> How can I create a family home?
>
> How do I break this goal down into steps?
>
> What can be my first step right now?

Changing the mindset away from earning money and more to working with nature to develop a sustainable life seems to be the key. However, Russia is in a strong position, with a vast amount of land. Not many countries have that much spare land that they can give away for such purposes. Furthermore, lots of people, still on a treadmill with their lives intertwined with all aspects of modern-day living, will find it hard to take such a big plunge (hence 99 per cent of people asking the wrong question). For those who can do this, it's fantastic. In fact, there is a similar policy here in the UK. In Wales, there is the One Planet Project, which will give people a piece of land if they are able to live an eco-friendly lifestyle. To apply, there are several criteria that need to be met, such as finding suitable land, having a management plan, evaluating and managing the land, building a zero energy home, growing food or rearing stock, setting up renewable energy supplies, and sourcing fresh water.

However, it's unrealistic to expect the majority of the population to move to this kind of model to avert climate change. Such policies should be encouraged and expanded, but the take-up will still be relatively low as a percentage of the world's population. As I write this book and think a family homestead would be an amazing thing, I just can't bring myself to drop my current lifestyle and make such a drastic change. I think I'm like a crack addict who's just discovered crack is bad for me. Just because an addict knows how bad it is, doesn't mean they will stop. They may try and stop, or they may reduce the amount of crack they take. If you stop abruptly, the withdrawal symptoms will be severe. It's the same with living in the modern world. For some, the transition to a natural way of living will need to be a gradual process. Many people live in a city, with a certain lifestyle and a family that's very settled; it's not so easy to give up everything and move to the countryside with no experience of living off the land.

Consequently, policies like the Wales One Planet Project and the Russian Family Homesteads are to be encouraged. But such policies need to be coupled with more practical things that people can do to transition to more eco-friendly lifestyles. For example, policies to encourage people to grow more of their own produce, such as making land available as allotments.

During lockdown, I read an article in my local paper that showed the top twenty-four items on people's bucket lists, which had changed in priority since lockdown.[51] I was overjoyed to see that at number one was growing their own vegetables. Just being in the list would have

---

51 Plymouth Herald, https://www.plymouthherald.co.uk/whats-on/whats-on-news/south-west-bucket-list-changes-4286818

been wonderful, but this was right at the top at number one. So if we had the right policies to promote growing our own produce, together with making land available for those with no gardens, then we could really start to make the transition. Carbon emissions would be cut, as would the use of large-scale machinery, harmful pesticides and fertilisers, and plastic packaging, and we would all be eating fresher and healthier produce. Yes, the economy would also be cut, but this doesn't make us worse off. We are better off by earning slightly less but also spending less and eating better.

Furthermore, we don't have to think of self-sufficiency being the only way to reduce the harmful effects of economic activity. Rather than doing things at a global level, we can do them at a national level. Or rather than doing things at a national level, we can do things at a local level. For example, we all know it's best to buy locally produced food where possible, reducing carbon emissions from food miles and keeping the food fresh. Well, the same applies to other trades too. The less we transport goods from one place to another, the more we reduce our carbon footprint. Keeping trade local can also benefit mental health, as there is more face-to-face interaction; when buying goods and services online, we often go without any human contact whatsoever.

As the world economy has become more and more global, we have seen different regions or countries become more and more specialised in what they do. By creating specialists in different areas, we have seen efficiencies in production. For example, London specialises in financial services, Silicon Valley in California specialises in technology, Bangladesh for textiles, China for manufacturing, Ghana for cocoa, and so on. By focusing on a smaller number of specialist goods and services, they get better at what they do. Collectively, we become more efficient and benefit from regional and international trade.

However, what this doesn't take into account is the breakdown in communities and the impact on the environment. As we buy goods and services from different corners of the globe, we lose the sense of community spirit. A community that is self-sufficient or nearly self-sufficient will have cohesion and a strong sense of identity, as everyone pulls together. When you get goods and services from other people, you will know them personally. Contrast that with a community where the vast majority of goods and services are produced elsewhere, often ordered and managed electronically, and never speaking to or meeting the people producing them. There may still be a community spirit, and there will even be communities crossing geographical boundaries, as people from different corners of the world interact. However, it will be much more fragmented and not as strong as one which is more self-sufficient and face-to-face.

Furthermore, the environmental impact of global trade and shipping goods from one place to another increases both the amount of packaging used and the carbon emissions from transportation. It also encourages international travel, often in business class, which has an extremely high carbon footprint.

CHAPTER 19

GOVERNMENT BUDGETS

When governments have financial difficulties as their expenditure exceeds their tax revenues, they seek a way to plug the gap. As they make their forecasts for the years ahead, they see economic growth as the solution. Instead of raising tax rates (which is unpopular), they forecast strong economic growth. As incomes of both individuals and companies grow, their tax revenues will grow, and this is seen as the best and least painful solution. However, what governments are not taking into account is the additional pressures that economic growth brings. Governments have at their disposal a tax revenue which is many times higher than what it was a few decades ago, and yet most still run budget deficits (where expenditure on government services exceeds income from tax revenue). There is a feeling that there just isn't enough money to produce the services that people require. Economic growth is actually part of the problem, as the new norms of society demand more and more; this excessive demand creates a multitude of problems.

Stop Stealing from Our Children

During hard times, a government may spend more than it receives in revenue, creating a budget deficit, and during good times, a government may spend less than it receives, creating a budget surplus. This is the basis of Keynesian economics, where over time, the deficits and surpluses would even out. However, today, despite being considerably richer than ever before, governments seem to be in a constant state of budget deficit. To put this in perspective, in 1980, government spending was £103bn; by 2019, that had risen to £854bn, and yet all government departments feel that they are being squeezed and need more money. Each year, the surplus or deficit can be seen as a percentage of GDP. Over the last forty years, there have been five surplus years, which in aggregate have totalled just 3 per cent of GDP. The thirty-five deficit years, by contrast, have totalled 140 per cent of GDP.[52] This doesn't include the year 2020, when the UK will have its biggest deficit ever, by far, due to the Covid-19 measures, which have massively reduced tax revenues and increased government spending. Governments will justify the higher borrowing levels as our GDP grows, but even as a percentage of GDP, total debt is double what it was in 1980.

Alternatively, they might say it's a good time to borrow more, as interest rates have become very low. They use this to justify spending on very large infrastructure projects, saying they are building for future generations, and it will increase GDP that will help service the debt. However, as we've seen from the vicious circles of economic growth, as GDP grows, the government (like individuals) will need to spend more on the new goods and services that the GDP has delivered on, and hence instead of having more tax revenues to pay the interest or repay the loans, they find themselves just spending more and more, and government finances will be even more squeezed.

---

[52] Countryeconomy.com, https://countryeconomy.com/deficit/uk

However, it is the future generations who will need to pay the taxes which service the loans that governments take out today, and although interest rates are very low now, who knows what they will be in one or two generations? Is it fair that we borrow to spend now for the benefit of ourselves, only for our children and grandchildren to be lumbered with the task of paying for such massive debt? When we run a budget deficit for a prolonged period, over a generation or more, we are effectively stealing from our children. We get to spend the money, but our children will have to pay it back with interest.

Furthermore, today we live in a world of increasing population, which helps to spread the burden of servicing rising levels of government debt. Whilst the forecast is for populations to continue to grow, population growth cannot continue indefinitely, and at some point, it will fall, due to the very limited resources and space available on planet earth. When it does, it will be even harder for our children to service the debt we have given them.

Three factors impact a nation's population: the birth rate, the death rate, and net immigration. If you take the UK, you could see how any one of these could cause a reduced population in future. The birth rate is already falling; in 2019, it was 12 per cent lower than it was in 2012, with the average woman only having 1.65 children.[53] As we discussed in chapter 5, an infectious disease more deadly than Covid-19 could possibly increase the death rate, and we seem to be doing everything we can to curb immigration. If the UK population is lower in one or two generations' time, there will be fewer taxpayers

---

[53] Office for National Statistics, https://www.ons.gov.uk/peoplepopulationand community/birthsdeathsandmarriages/livebirths/bulletins/birthsummary tablesenglandandwales/2019

to pay the interest on outstanding government debt, which is already equivalent to £28k per person, or £98k per household.[54]

Lastly, the ability of our children and grandchildren to pay back the ever-rising government debt levels is heavily dependent on future economic growth. If you are still reading this book, then I hope by now I have convinced you that this is neither sustainable nor desirable. If we manage to shrink the monetary economy in favour of the natural economy, how can we expect future generations to repay such large levels of government debt?

Investing in Infrastructure

The massive infrastructure projects that governments embark on require borrowing many extra billions of pounds, destroying natural habitats, creating pollution, and adding to the climate change crisis, all of which will need to be paid for and cleaned up by future generations. For example, at the time of writing (2020), the UK government has earmarked £27bn for infrastructure spending, including four thousand miles of new roads.[55] However, according to the Campaign for Better Transport, "When a new road is built, new traffic will divert onto it. Many people may make new trips they would otherwise not make, and will travel longer distances just because of the presence of the new road."[56] If having more roads encourages more car journeys, then having fewer roads will encourage fewer

---

[54] Based on figures from the Office for National Statistics, government debt of £1.877bn as at June 2020, UK population of 66.8m in mid-2019, and 19.2 million families in 2019.

[55] The Guardian, 11 March 2020, https://www.theguardian.com/uk-news/2020/mar/11/chancellor-announces-27bn-for-roadbuilding-in-budget

[56] Campaign for Better Transport, https://bettertransport.org.uk/roads-nowhere/induced-traffic

auto trips. So instead of building more roads, how about a more radical transport policy, like repurposing existing roads for cycle paths? If we were to repurpose just 1 per cent of UK roads from cars to bikes, there would be twenty-six hundred miles of fabulous, wide cycle paths created for free. Alternatively, on roads with multiple lanes, one lane could be repurposed for wider pavements for walking and cycling paths. There would be a few roads that would initially get busier, but if chosen carefully, for many journeys, you could ditch the car in favour of a bike. For example, finding commuter journeys where there is more than one possible route, if one route was repurposed for cycling, then many would be persuaded to take the bike to work, either because they love the idea of cycling to work on a traffic free road, or because the other roads are too busy. Such a policy would be almost free to implement, people would become fitter, the air would become less polluted, our carbon footprint would be reduced, and biodiversity would increase. The principal reason why such policies are not pushed is because they don't add to GDP. In fact, they reduce it because we are spending less on cars and fuel, which are more expensive than cycling. Governments would rather build extra roads and extra cycle paths, both of which add to GDP.

What Drives Government Policy?

We have already talked about the concentration of wealth in the hands of the few, specifically the top 1 per cent. One other problem with this is that the economic elite have a great deal of power and pull the strings of governments. According to Thomas Ferguson, an American political scientist, when big businesses make contributions to political parties, they do so because they expect a return on their investment in the form of favourable policies. He says if you trace the finance backing any major political campaign, you'll see what drives its policies.[57] It will be big businesses that fear these policy suggestions the most, so it won't be a surprise when all the major political parties resist them. Again, money is the problem. Politicians who may have gone into politics for the right reasons, to change the world for what they believe in, end up implementing policies which are funded by the super-rich, in order to stay in power.

---

[57] Thomas Ferguson, *Golden Rule: The Investment Theory of Party Competition and the Logic of Money-Driven Political Systems.*

CHAPTER 20

TIPPING POINT

There is a tipping point when the amount of damage we do to the environment is going to have a catastrophic impact to the planet and to ourselves, and the damage done will be irreversible. We are very close to that point. Environmental activists like Greta Thunberg have pointed this out, as have many scientists. With so many variables, we don't know exactly when we will reach it, but we do know it's soon; the general consensus is around the year 2030, which is not very far way. First, let me try to explain how climate change activists have concluded 2030 is a sensible estimate for D-Day. As global temperatures rise due to human activity, in about ten years, the ice in the Arctic will have melted during summer months. Currently, the ice reflects the sun's rays, keeping temperatures down, so if the ice melts, this cooling effect disappears, and the earth starts to heat up even faster. Then the soil in the north will start to melt, releasing methane into the atmosphere. Methane is a greenhouse gas that has a far greater impact on climate than the carbon dioxide that we have been releasing into the atmosphere, so again, the earth will heat up more and at a much faster rate. This in turn heats up the oceans further, and as they become more acidic, due to the additional carbon dioxide we produce, which gets dissolved in the oceans, coral reefs die, and the fish population plummets. These increased temperatures will also bring about extreme weather conditions such as flooding, heatwaves, droughts, and storms.

Not only will this cause death and destruction on a mass scale for both humans and wildlife, but coupled with the degradation that the soil will have suffered due to our intensive farming methods and overuse of fertilisers, it is easy to see that we won't be able to grow enough produce to feed ourselves. Even financial markets are starting to recognise the risk of climate change, as climate risks can have significant financial implications for a firm's valuation. Recent research by Phillip Krueger has discovered that "fewer than 10% of investors believe that climate risks will materialise only in ten years or beyond,"[58] so even financial markets are predicting that climate change will start harming businesses within a decade.

---

[58] European Corporate Governance Institute, https://ecgi.global/sites/default/files/working_papers/documents/finalkruegersautnerstarks_0.pdf

Climate Change Timeline

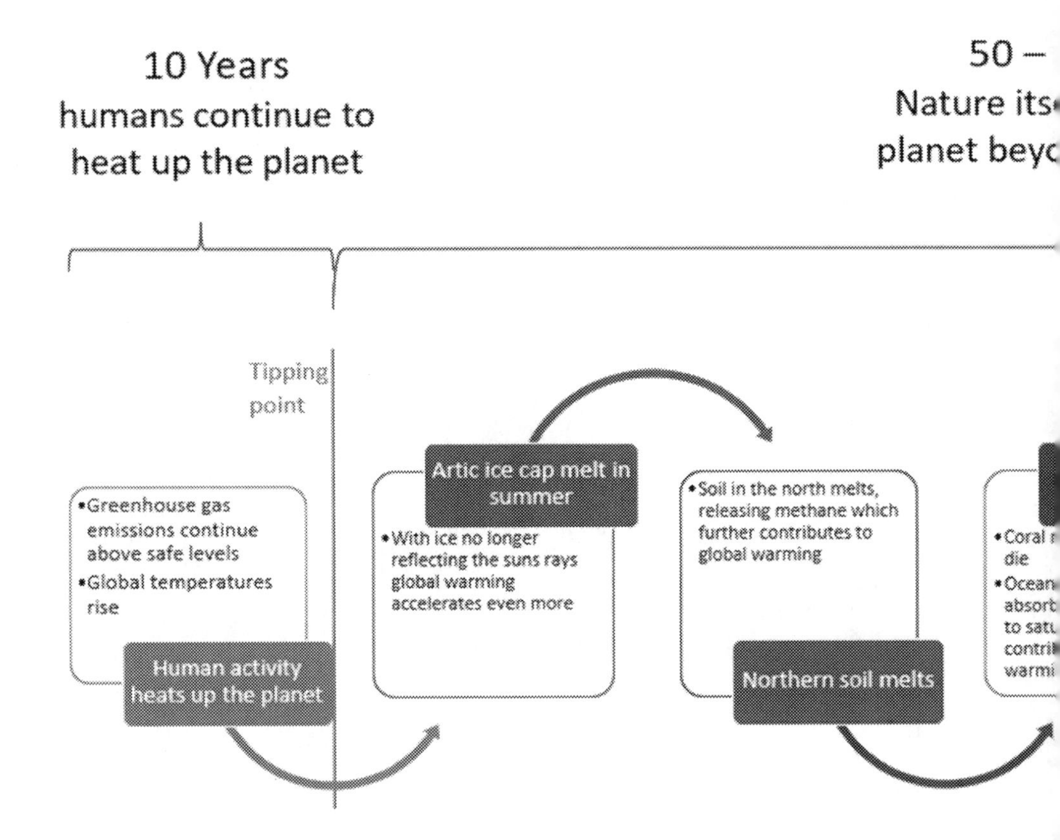

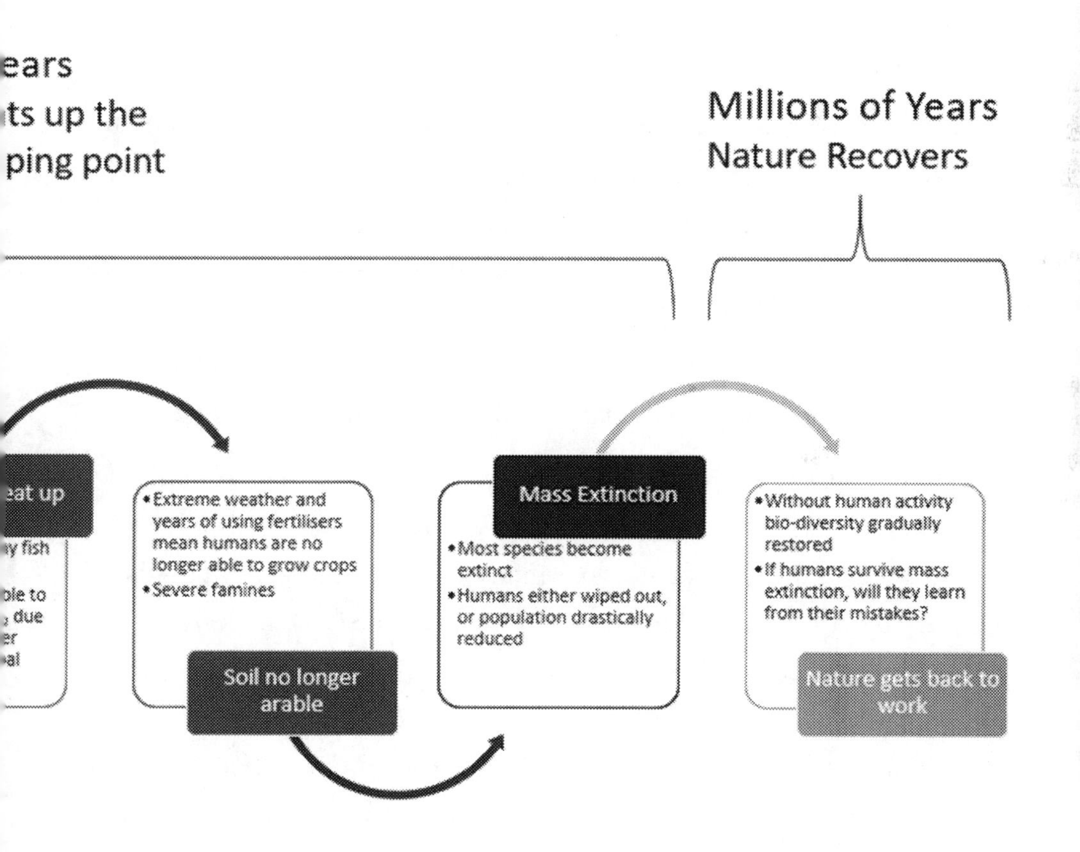
ears
ts up the
ping point
Millions of Years
Nature Recovers
eat up
Extreme weather and years of using fertilisers mean humans are no longer able to grow crops
Severe famines
Soil no longer arable
Mass Extinction
Most species become extinct
Humans either wiped out, or population drastically reduced
Without human activity bio-diversity gradually restored
If humans survive mass extinction, will they learn from their mistakes?
Nature gets back to work

These feedback loops, where the rising temperature of the planet creates yet more heating, are just some of the issues scientists have discovered. How many more are there that we don't yet understand? With the loss of biodiversity that will result from increased temperatures, both on land and in our oceans, there will be many more implications that we cannot predict. As we've discussed, nature is so interconnected that such a loss of biodiversity will further throw the natural equilibrium of our planet out of balance.

This is extremely serious, yet most people just don't seem to understand the gravity of the situation. And yet climate change is only one potential catastrophe that we are facing. Alternatively, our disregard for nature may produce a different disaster, such as another infectious disease outbreak. With Covid-19, the virus had a very low mortality rate, but if the next one is just as infectious but far more deadly, it could wipe out a large percentage of the population.

With the Covid-19 outbreak, it's interesting to see people's attitude towards risk when it comes to their own life or the lives of their loved ones; some are risk-takers, but many more are risk-averse. This is very understandable, but why can't we apply the same logic when the stakes are much higher, like the health of the planet and civilisation as we know it? The damage we are doing to the environment is already killing far more people than Covid-19. The Guardian reported that in 2018, around 8.7 million deaths were caused by fossil fuels – that's about 4 times as many that died of Covid-19 in 2020. In addition to the deaths, they also reported that the use of fossil fuels causes heart disease, respiratory ailments and even the loss of eyesight with the associated global economic and health costs amounting to $2.9tn.[59]

---

[59] The Guardian 9 February 2021 https://www.theguardian.com/environment/2021/feb/09/fossil-fuels-pollution-deaths-research

Why should a slow death from pollution be less important than a quick death from Covid-19?

A possibility of death in two or three weeks (Covid-19) may seem more immediate than a possibility of death in two or three decades (climate change). However, with climate change on the horizon, the probability of death (and many other devastating impacts on our lives) is much higher than the 1 to 2 per cent chance of dying from Covid-19 (and that's if you're one of the unlucky few who catch it), and it will be on a scale that is catastrophic, making the impacts of Covid-19 seem like a mild cold. Bill Gates warns that climate change will be worse than Covid-19 if we don't act now, noting that the reduction in emissions we have seen from the pandemic as a result of reduced travel would not be enough.[60] We plan for the future by putting money into a pension scheme to prepare for a retirement several decades in the future, so we should be petrified about the prospect of a climate change catastrophe that could happen before many of us retire, and we should do everything in our power to avoid it.

So why don't we? We declared a climate change emergency in 2019, but two years on, we are still not acting like it's an emergency. When the world was hit by the Covid-19 pandemic, governments imposed extreme measures to do everything they could to stop the spread of the virus. The world as we knew it ground to a halt, and the situation was treated with the gravity and urgency of a true emergency. We follow the advice of the ministers who lead us, who don't seem to be extremely concerned with drastic change that would cripple the monetary economy; after all, saving lives is more important than saving money.

---

60 CNBC, 8 January 2021, https://www.cnbc.com/2021/01/08/bill-gates-climate-change-could-be-worse-than-covid-19.html

Imagine if the government imposed regulations to curb climate change on the same scale as they did with the pandemic. They wouldn't even need to be as extreme as the Covid-19 lockdown measures we accepted; for example, just curbing nonessential travel, which uses fossil fuels, would be a start and much less harsh than the isolating lockdowns we endured. Imagine what the government slogan might be: "Walk & Cycle, Eat Plants, Save the Planet." I'm sure you can you think of a better one; send your ideas to me (contact details at the end of the book). There is no doubt that individuals would begin to care about climate catastrophe if it meant their lives and liberties were restricted directly by government policy. But politicians instead choose to act unconcerned, fearing unpopularity with their corrupt sponsors.

In the last forty years, we have cut down 1 billion hectares of forests, equivalent to a woodland the size of Europe. We are emitting 4 billion tons of CO_2 into the atmosphere in a year. We consume over 300 million tons of meat each year, which require over 2 trillion tons of water. The world temperature is rising. 700 billion tons of ice are being melted in a year. Sea levels are rising.[61] I could go on, but it's not difficult to see the chilling picture: The tipping point is approaching fast.

Most people understand the problem, and some will do their bit to slightly modify their life to reduce their impact on the environment when they can. However, not enough people are taking the more drastic action needed to avoid a catastrophe. I believe part of the reason for this is a catastrophe can only be averted if there is a united effort, not just at an individual, family, community, regional, or even national level, but on a global scale. So the attitude of many will be

[61] The World Counts, https://www.theworldcounts.com

that there is no point taking such drastic action to their own lives, when several other billion people around the world just carry on living as normal, or only moderate their lives slightly.

The individual impact that each of us can make is minuscule, so it's understandable why people don't take drastic action. However, I do believe that if we get the right direction from the leaders of this world, then most people would welcome this and move towards a greener, more sustainable lifestyle. Each person has around 1.6 hectares of the earth's resources to use. If policies direct people to take no more than their fair share of the earth's resources, then people will see this as both equitable and responsible.

Tipping points are not always easy to see. When the stress on the edge of a geologic fault reaches its tipping point, it creates an earthquake, but it's not easy to spot. The build-up of mortgages caused the 2008 financial crisis, but not many anticipated it; even the Queen asked why no one saw it coming. Well, in the case of climate change, decades ago, scientists predicting a catastrophe may have been in their minority, but today, there is no hiding from it. Most of us accept it's coming unless we take drastic action, so let's act now, as individuals, as corporations, and as governments in unison across the globe. Furthermore, in the UK, we should not say there is no point in being environmentally friendly unless China, India and the US do so as well. We may have a relatively small impact, but we still have a big voice. We need to lead by example, not shirk our responsibilities.

CHAPTER 21

SUMMARY

Nature is our biggest ally and our greatest inspiration.
—David Attenborough

I think we all know we need to work with nature, not against it. The single biggest incentive we have to deviate from nature and propel the planet into destruction is our economic policies which drive us to earn more and consume more. Over the course of this book, I hope that I have convinced you to re-evaluate the extent to which industrial modern living is beneficial for us and for the planet, and to consider the advantages of moving towards a more equal, more communal, and more natural way of life. I hope that this book demonstrates how urgently we need to change the goal posts away from economic growth and begin to consider the value of the natural economy, alongside the existing monetary one.

In terms of tangible recommendations for governments, the ideas in this book are actually quite simple:

Policy	Impact
Change the goal	Reduce the importance of GDP and other financial metrics. Instead, focus on metrics which boost nature, rather than the economy, such as air quality, water quality, soil quality reducing greenhouse gas emissions and food miles. They are plenty more to choose from.
Share the wealth	Take a global view to taxing corporate profits to close loopholes and increase corporate tax rates. Then redistribute this income, enabling others to pursue a more self-sufficient, environmentally friendly lifestyle, and bringing developing countries out of poverty, which will stabilise the world population
Sin taxes	Make environmentally unfriendly goods and service prohibitively expensive, incentivising a transition to healthy lives; a plant-based diet to free up land, clean air, clean water, clean oceans, clean energy, and fertile soil; and raise more money to fund a universal income
Repurpose the land	With land made available from our changing diets, make it accessible for rewilding projects, allotments, and kin domains

There is cause to be optimistic. As we come out of the pandemic, many are calling for a green recovery, seeing this as a unique opportunity to invest in renewable energy and move away from fossil fuels. And this includes mainstream politicians, not just the green ones. And behind the scenes policy makers are waking up to the idea that our current economic framework is not sustainable. For example, the UK government recently commissioned an independent report on The Economics of Biodiversity[62]. The report was led by led by Professor Sir Partha Dasgupta and concluded that 'We have collectively failed to engage with Nature sustainably, to the extent that our demands far exceed its capacity to supply us with the goods and services

62 Final Report - The Economics of Biodiversity: The Dasgupta Review https://www.gov.uk/government/publications/final-report-the-economics-of-biodiversity-the-dasgupta-review?fbclid=IwAR0kWZ8_GUuPvy3aemgIGOvDuw1K8bnf7yqKRwLtXZk25YvACOpOHJ1Hqq0

we all rely on', and 'Our unsustainable engagement with Nature is endangering the prosperity of current and future generations'. The report concedes that GDP does not take account of the nature as an asset, and that a measure of success needs to include it. They even concede that 'The devastating impacts of COVID-19 and other emerging infectious diseases – of which land-use change and species exploitation are major drivers – could prove to be just the tip of the iceberg if we continue on our current path'.

Governments and policy makers seem to be waking up to the idea that multinational corporations are paying to little, and things need to change. In the March 2021 UK budget, it was announced that corporation tax would increase to 25 per cent in 2023, and that this higher rate would not apply to businesses with profits under £50k. This would be the first increase in corporation tax for several decades. The ideas of changing the formula so that businesses are assessed on their global profits also seems to be gaining traction, as is the concept of a universal income. Combined, these give the possibility of a considerable redistribution of wealth to reverse the ever widening gap between rich and poor.

Furthermore, the global response to COVID-19 shows that all countries and all people are capable of making drastic changes to policies and lifestyles if required. For example, the idea of doubling or tripling the price of aviation travel to combat air pollution and climate change may previously have seemed outrageous, but it's actually a lot less harsh that the near outright ban on flying imposed to combat COVID-19.

However, I don't intend to leave you, as a reader, feeling helpless, like you simply have to wait around for the government to act. Many of the greatest revolutions in history began with grassroots pressure from the people. If there are ideas in this book that you like, you could write to your local politician. Also look out for petitions asking for such changes, then sign them and share them. United, we can demand change that will ensure a better future for our children, our grandchildren, and our beautiful planet.

In addition to these government policies, there are of course steps we can take in our own lives as individuals. Here are some questions to ask yourself:

- Do I really need to take that journey, and if I do, what's the most environmentally friendly way I can make it?
- Do I really need that new piece of clothing, and if I do, could I buy second-hand?
- Are there more eco-friendly products that I could use for washing, cleaning, and personal care, and could I use less of them?
- Could I cut back on meat and dairy consumption and eat more plant-based foods, even if it's just for one or two meals a week?
- Do I have the opportunity to grow any of my own produce?
- Could I buy produce that is grown more locally?
- Could I waste less food and recycle food in a compost bin?
- Before I put something in the bin, ask can I recycle it, or if it's broken, can I mend it?
- Can I cut down on single-use plastics?
- If I invest money, can I invest it in eco-friendly products and technology?
- Is my energy supplier 100 per cent renewable?
- What can I do to my home to make it more eco-friendly: solar panels, solar thermal, heat pumps, biomass boilers,

insulation, low-energy lighting? Some can be expensive, but worth considering if, say, replacing your boiler.

- Can I switch to an electric car or, better still, ditch the car?
- Can I entertain myself with nature, like a day at the beach, instead of in a commercial environment, like a shopping centre or cinema?
- Can I work less?
- Can I outsource less?
- Can I cook at home more instead of using ready-made meals, buying takeaways, or eating out?
- Could I take a packed lunch or a flask of coffee instead of buying them on the go?

The list is endless; we just have to keep asking ourselves what we could do differently. If you are doing something which simplifies your life, reduces your work, or reduces your consumption, it's probably going to be good for the environment. Be confident in the knowledge that our own individual decisions do make a difference. Even if it feels like a drop in the ocean, feel empowered that you are taking a stance for the greater good.

The policy suggestions outlined in this book may well have some flaws, and there may be better alternative policies to implement. However, I hope this contributes to the thinking behind a growing call for a more radical approach to economics to benefit both humans and the planet alike. Furthermore, I think you can see that it's not difficult to make a very substantial difference to the environment by making bold changes to the way we govern ourselves, rather than tinkering with the existing system so as not to upset anyone. So I can only hope this generates the debate required to make real changes in government policies in the UK and around the globe, shifting the political objectives away from exponential economic growth and towards sustainable, natural lifestyles, supported by taxation and benefits that enable a fairer distribution of wealth.

When history looks back at today, if we choose monetary value over our beautiful planet, we will never be forgiven. Let's do the right thing: If we take care of nature, nature will take care of us.

Printed in the United States
by Baker & Taylor Publisher Services